Nancy Tamarisk

Once Upon a Time

Once Upon a Time

A short history of fairy tale

MARINA WARNER

OXFORD
UNIVERSITY PRESS

OXFORD
UNIVERSITY PRESS

Great Clarendon Street, Oxford, OX2 6DP,
United Kingdom

Oxford University Press is a department of the University of Oxford.
It furthers the University's objective of excellence in research, scholarship,
and education by publishing worldwide. Oxford is a registered trade mark of
Oxford University Press in the UK and in certain other countries

Published in the United States of America by Oxford University Press
198 Madison Avenue, New York, NY 10016, United States of America

British Library Cataloguing in Publication Data
Data available

Library of Congress Control Number: 2014940242

ISBN 978–0–19–871865–9

Printed in Italy by
L.E.G.O. S.p.A.

To Carolina, Riccardo, Sofia, and Hartley
(tesoro meraviglioso)

CONTENTS

Contents

ACKNOWLEDGEMENTS

I have been thinking about fairy tales for a while, and friends, students, and colleagues have asked questions and made comments that have helped me hugely and crucially in the making of this book. For ten years, I've taught courses on fairy tales, given classes and talks, and written articles on various aspects of the topic. I would like to thank everyone who has invited me to speak, come to hear me, raised or discussed issues with me, and I offer heartfelt gratitude in particular to Jack Zipes, the well-named hero of fairy tale studies and mentor to so many readers and scholars; to Donald Haase, Cristina Bacchilega, and Anne Duggan, editors of the journal *Marvels & Tales*; Martine Hennard-Dutheil at the University of Lausanne; Daniela Corona and Valentina Castagna at the University of Palermo; Hilary Ballon of New York University, Abu Dhabi; Val Morgan, Peter Hulme, Jonathan Lichtenstein, Philip Terry, Karin Littau, Elizabeth Kuti, Adrian May, and Sanja Bahun at the University of Essex; Kevin Dawson of Whistledown Productions; Mary-Kay Wilmers, editor of the *London Review of Books*; to Andrea Keegan, and others among many editors at Oxford University Press, for their patience over the years it took; and to Beatrice Dillon for her help throughout, especially in the thickets of the cyberwood.

To Graeme Segal, believer in another kind of other world (that of mathematical reality), my love and endless thanks.

ILLUSTRATIONS

PROLOGUE

The Prospect

Imagine the history of fairy tale as a map, like the Carte du Tendre, the 'Map of Tenderness', drawn by Parisian romancers to chart the peaks and sloughs of the heart's affections: unfurl this imaginary terrain in your mind's eye, and you will first see two prominent landmarks, Charles Perrault's *Histoires et Contes du temps passé* (Tales of Olden Times, 1697) and a little nearer in the foreground, the Grimm Brothers' *Kinder- und Hausmärchen* (Children's and Household Tales, 1812–57). These collections dominate their surroundings so imposingly that they make it hard to pick out other features near or far.

Gradually, however, as your eyes adjust to the dazzle, several more features of the scene begin to grow in definition and give you better bearings: along a whole web of routes from points further east, *The Tales of the Thousand and One Nights* form deep aquifers of story running through the entire expanse, and emerging here and there in waterfalls and powerful rivers spreading through wide floodplains. Harbours and market-places and pilgrimage sites—Venice,

Naples, Genoa, Sicily, in Italy alone—begin to emerge as significant centres of talkative storytelling populations.

To the north, Hans Christian Andersen's glowing Danish homeland is emitting powerful signals from regions stretching to the Arctic circle; and when your eyes track his large force field, you begin to discover beacons blazing in the darkness, lit by the work of Walter Scott in Scotland, Alexander Afanasyev in Russia, and other omnivores of their countries' stories. The circumpolar regions, as well as the steppes and forests of Russia and Central Asia, are also rich in fairy tale ore: the ogress Baba Yaga lives deep in the forest in a hut that runs around on chicken legs, loves to eat children (but plucky Vasilissa the Beautiful foils the witch's plans, see Figure 1). Baba Yaga, like her counterparts farther south, sometimes takes a more innocent fancy to one of the heroes or heroines, and showers them with boons and blessings.

If you could turn this fictive atlas into an advent calendar and open windows in the scenery, you would then see scores of storytellers and inventors gathering, interpreting, re-visioning the material—hidden away hard at work in Ireland are Speranza Wilde and her son Oscar, W. B. Yeats and his patron Lady Gregory; in Wales, Charlotte Guest, who established the first English *Mabinogion*, a treasury of marvellous stories; in Zurich and Vienna, Carl Jung and Sigmund Freud; in Toronto, Japan, and South London, Margaret Atwood and Angela Carter. In full view and in close-up, windows that are in fact not windows but movie screens are shimmering with the works of inspired adaptors—Jean Cocteau with *La Belle et la bête* (1946), a poetic, slow-moving romance that crystallizes the seductive mysterious eros at the heart of fairy tale. Film adaptors and producers, stage directors, and designers are busy refashioning fairy tales for audiences of all ages, creating theatrical spectacles that combine circus techniques, masking, song and dance in the raucous and sentimental lineage of pantomime. Therapists, performance artists, couturiers, and photographers . . . a festive cavalcade of those professions now called 'creative content providers' are losing themselves in the forests of fairy tale in order to come back with baskets of strawberries picked in the snow.

There remain many more windows to open; in fact they're numberless, and besides it becomes clear that the scenery is not stable, for the land masses and landmarks are floating in a vast ocean, the Ocean of Story, which, like the cosmic river of the ancient world, encircles the earth since recorded time. The light keeps changing over the scene, now plunging a once prominent element into shadow, then turning its beam on another hitherto disregarded part of the territory.

Stories slipped across frontiers of culture and language as freely as birds in the air as soon as they first began appearing; fairy tales migrate on soft feet, for borders are invisible to them, no matter how ferociously they are policed by cultural purists.

The Ocean of Story is the title of one of the most ancient collections of fairy tales—a phrase Salman Rushdie adapted for his fable, *Haroun and the Sea of Stories*. We swim, float, or navigate this fluid and marvellous body of water as a matter of course; mass media, television, game shows, video games, and every kind of popular entertainment trawl it daily to bring up plots and characters, animals and motifs.

This map of fairy tales still contains many unexplored corners and much terra incognita, and eagerness to discover new parts of it is growing among different audiences. Considered children's literature for a dominant period of their history, fairy tales have now grown out of that Victorian and Edwardian prescription and have gained a new stature over the last twenty years, both as inspiration for literature, and for mass, lucrative entertainment. Thematic and structural similarities continue to attach contemporary fictions to popular and ancient legends and myths. Fairy tales are one of their dominant expressions, connective tissue between a mythological past and the present realities.

The Thorny Hedge: Questions of Definition

What are the defining characteristics of a fairy tale? First, 'a fairy tale' is a short narrative, sometimes less than a single page, sometimes running to many more, but the term no longer applies, as it once did, to a novel-length work. Secondly, fairy tales are familiar stories, either verifiably old because they have been passed on down the generations or because the listener or reader is struck by their family resemblance to another story; they can appear pieced and patched, like an identikit photofit. The genre belongs in the general realm of folklore, and many fairy tales are called 'folk tales', and are attributed to oral tradition, and considered anonymous and popular in the sense of originating not among an élite, but among the unlettered, the *Volk* (the people in German, as in 'Volkswagen', the 'People's Car'). The accumulated wisdom of the past has been deposited in them—at least, that is the feeling a fairy tale radiates and the claim the form has made since the first collections. Scholars of fairy tales distinguish between genuine folk tales (*Märchen*) and literary or 'arty' fairy tales (*Kunstmärchen*); the first are customarily anonymous and undatable, the latter signed and dated, but the history of the stories' transmission shows inextricable and fruitful entanglement.

Even when every effort was made to keep the two branches apart, fairy tales would insist on becoming literature. On the stage, a similar, traditional sense of an ancient, oral voice sounds in the libretto or plot: Tchaikovsky's *Swan Lake*, Bartók and Balász's *Bluebeard's Castle*, Dvořák's mermaid opera *Rusalka*, or a Ballets Russes production such as *Firebird*, proclaim their roots in unauthored folklore, although they are in themselves unique and original works. Cinema likewise announces its proximity to tradition—while often claiming implicitly to be filling out the original in the most effective and satisfactory possible way, cinema being the *Gesamtkunstwerk* (the total work of art) with the largest audience. One television series of fairy tales was simply called *The Storyteller* (1988). Written and directed by Anthony Minghella with the puppeteer Jim Henson, each episode opened with a fireside scene in which a storyteller, played by John Hurt, dramatized the fairy tale we were about to watch, presenting it as part of a living tradition come down through the centuries. In fact, these versions are some of the most adventurous and inventive variations on the material ever made for television.

Second-order narrative of this kind, which is not ashamed to proclaim its fidelity to the past, diverges fundamentally from the cultural ideals, in fiction and other forms of creation, of singularity and novelty. The Grimms wanted to uncover the true voice of the German *Volk* by transcribing fairy tales from oral sources; they made a pretence of vanishing from their opus. Angela Carter (1941–92) saw the matter differently. She declared she wanted to put new wine in old bottles so that they would explode. But the old bottles were necessary to create her fantastic pyrotechnics.

A third defining characteristic of fairy tales follows organically from the implied oral and popular tradition: the necessary presence of the past makes itself felt through combinations and recombinations of familiar plots and characters, devices and images; they might be attached to a particular well-known fairy tale—such as 'Puss-in-Boots' or 'Cinderella'—but fairy tales are generically recognizable even when the exact identity of the particular story is not clear. A universe of faerie is the matrix for any number of incidents that take place within its borders, incidents which then bud and effloresce into fairy tales as such, discrete and interwoven. The term 'fairytale' is often used as an epithet—a fairytale setting, a fairytale ending—for a work that is not in itself a fairy tale, because it depends on elements of the form's symbolic language. *Fairytale* or, sometimes, *faery* or *faerie* (as in Edmund Spenser's allegory *The Faerie Queene*) or 'fairy' (Joseph Addison in 1712 wrote of 'the Fairy Way of Writing') are epithets applied to evoke a quality of a scene or figure beyond *a fairy tale* as a distinct narrative. For example, an episode in an epic (Circe turning men into swine marks her as the predecessor of the wicked witch). Elements in many of the great Victorian and Edwardian children's stories have a fairytale character. The authors of newly invented stories, such as Charles Dickens and Charles Kingsley, George Eliot, E. Nesbit, and J. R. R. Tolkien, do not write fairy tales as such, but they adopt and transform recognizable elements—flying carpets, magic rings, animals that talk—from fairytale conventions, adding to readers' enjoyment by the direct appeal to shared knowledge of the fantasy code.

Fourthly, the scope of fairy tale is made by language: fairy tale consists above all of acts of imagination, conveyed in a symbolic Esperanto; its building blocks include certain kinds of characters (stepmothers and princesses, elves and giants) and certain recurrent motifs (keys, apples, mirrors, rings, and toads); the symbolism comes alive and communicates meaning through imagery of strong contrasts and sensations, evoking simple, sensuous phenomena that glint and sparkle, pierce and flow, by these means striking recognition in the reader or listener's body at a visceral depth (glass and forests; gold and silver; diamonds and rubies; thorns and knives; wells and tunnels). The novelist A. S. Byatt calls this 'the narrative grammar'. Byatt is herself a brilliantly combinatorial creator of stories from this repertory, and shows her attraction to this prime material of fairy tale when she writes of the Grimm Brothers:

> It is interesting how impossible it is to remember a time when my head was not full of these unreal people, things, and events...The Tales...are older, simpler, and deeper than the individual imagination.
>
> It is very odd, when you come to think of it—that human beings in all sorts of societies, ancient and modern, have

> needed these untrue stories . . . These 'flat' stories appear to be
> there because stories are a pervasive and perpetual human
> characteristic, like language, like play.

Fairy tales are one-dimensional, depthless, abstract, and sparse;
their characteristic manner is matter-of-fact—describing a
wolf devouring a young girl, ordering a palace chef to cook a
young woman, or chopping up a child to make blood pudding
arouses no cry of protest or horror from the teller. This is as it is,
as it happened; the tale is as it is, no more no less.

The conventional character of the repertory that typifies
fairy tales has inspired scholars to draft various systems to
capture it. The Russian formalists codified the stories: Vladimir Propp in his *Morphology of the Folktale* (1928) produced a
grid; he argues that there are so many characters and functions and plots, and many of the structuralist terms he used,
such as 'animal helper', have become standard (though the
numbers he determined have proved elastic). Folklorists in
Scandinavia, with many adherents in Germany, worked on
the remarkable Aarne-Thompson-Uther index of tale types
and its companion magnum opus, the *Motif-Index*; these
great encyclopaedic works tabulate and cross-reference
every component of fairy tales on record. But the work can
never be done, and currently the established taxonomy is
growing to include motifs and plots from the *Nights* and
from other cultures' multifarious bodies of storytelling.
Such work produces databases of great usefulness, especially
for cross-cultural comparison and pattern recognition; these
databases are monuments of literary archaeology, and they

prefigured the age of computers and the current fashion for combinatorial archiving of narrative, as they juggle the units in play in fairy tales. But, as in the fabulist Jorge Luis Borges' brilliant short tale 'On Exactitude in Science', in which the map grows to encompass every detail of the terrain until it becomes the size of the land it represents, these indices are ultimately self-defeating. The insight they give into what makes fairy tales compelling is limited: the universalizing method which ipso facto looks for resemblances, not distinctiveness, erases historical and social conditions; the comparisons and sets do not allow for differences in reception according to changing contexts, and they give no clue to the pleasure the fairy tales inspire or the reasons for that pleasure.

In a fine essay of 1939, 'On Fairy-Stories', Tolkien stepped into the kitchen: 'Speaking of the history of stories and especially of fairy-stories we may say that the Pot of Soup, the Cauldron of Story, has always been boiling, and to it have continually been added new bits, dainty and undainty ... If we speak of a Cauldron, we must not wholly forget the Cooks. There are many things in the Cauldron, but the Cooks do not dip in the ladle quite blindly.' Angela Carter picked up the metaphor more pithily: 'Who first invented meatballs? In what country? Is there a definitive recipe for potato soup? Think in terms of the domestic arts. This is how *I* make potato soup.' By contrast, the Czech poet Miroslav Holub reached for a biblical analogy: he compared writing to the miracle in the New Testament, when Jairus calls out to Jesus to help his 12-year-old daughter. Jesus enters the house only to find that the child has already died, but he comes out and tells the family and friends gathered there that she's merely sleeping. And so it turns out.

What Holub means is that literature is always a resurrected body, or a body that is continuously being resurrected. Its continual survival depends on its transformations.

Another alternative term for 'fairy tale' is 'wonder tale', from the German *Wundermärchen*, and it catches a quality of the genre more eloquently than 'fairy tale' or 'folk tale'. Although it does not enjoy the currency of 'fairy tale', 'wonder tale' recognizes the ubiquitousness of magic in the stories. The suspension of natural physical laws produces a magical state of reality throughout this form of narrative, which leads to wonder, astonishment, *'ajaib*, as invoked by Arabic literary ideas of fairy tale. Supernatural agency and the pleasure of wonder are interwoven in the character of fairy tales—this interrelationship presents a fifth defining characteristic.

Wonders shape plots that promise all kinds of riches; fairy tales are 'consolatory fables', the term the great Italian novelist and editor of fairy tales Italo Calvino (1936–85) uses, and they typically offer hope of release from poverty, maltreatment, and subjection. A happy ending is one of their generic markers. The American scholar Harold Bloom, reflecting on the function of imagery, relates it to the concoctions of fairy worlds and their promises: 'We welcome literary metaphor,' he has written, 'because it enables fictions to persuade us of beautiful untrue things…I tend to define metaphor as a figure of desire rather than a figure of knowledge.' Fairy tales report from imaginary territory—a magical elsewhere of possibility; a hero or a heroine or sometimes both together are faced with ordeals, terrors, and disaster in a world that, while it bears some resemblance to the ordinary conditions of human existence, mostly diverges from it in the way it works, taking the protagonists—and us, the story's readers or listeners—to another place where wonders are commonplace and desires are fulfilled. André Jolles's comment is sharply perceptive: 'The miraculous is here the only possible guarantee that the immorality of reality has stopped.'

The imaginary place and an imaginary time, constituted by magic and wonders performed by beings who have powers to enchant, are essential to this act of symbolic projection, and so a sixth defining characteristic of the genre can be placed under the heading of 'the happy ending': fairy tales express hopes. The agents who bring about miracles of hope in the stories vary from place to place, as they rise from local belief systems which belong to tradition. The tradition may contain imaginary elements but also traces of history: fairies and goblins on the one hand, cunning beldames and stepmothers on the other. The history is itself often an imagined history: King Arthur inspired romances that in turn carry into fairy tales motifs and plot devices—enchanted objects (swords, mirrors, cups), tests and riddles, dangers from monsters and forests, dream journeys, and a sense of the other world near to hand. The actions of such distant predecessors then add to the sum of knowledge of our situation now; from a distance, the other zone throws light on circumstances in the one we know. Fairy tales evoke every kind of violence, injustice, and mischance, but in order to declare it need not continue.

Angela Carter called the spirit of fairy tale 'heroic opti-mism', a better phrase for the promise of the happy ending. Others identify it as blind hope, or as wishful thinking, the life principle in action. It carries the tales of terrible dark deeds to their unlikely conclusion. There is the occasional well-known fairy tale that ends badly, like 'Red Riding Hood' according to Charles Perrault. But it is an aberration, as shown by myriad popular variations in which the young girl tricks the wolf out of his prize or even kills him herself. The most often told version introduces a hero: the Grimms brought her father into the plot.

You have a sketch map and a rough guide; the lights are lit in the windows of that house in the deep dark forest ahead of us. We can begin to move in, listening out, eyes open, trying to find our bearings.

1

The Worlds of Faery

Far Away & Down Below

Up the airy mountain,
Down the rushy glen,
We daren't go a-hunting
For fear of little men;
Wee folk, good folk,
Trooping all together;
Green jacket, red cap,
And white owl's feather!

William Allingham, 'Rewards and Fairies'

Few people believe in fairies, now, but they featured power-fully in the belief systems of the past, and not always benignly. Like witches, fairies have inspired fears that led to terrible acts, and not in only pre-modern societies far away, but ones closer to hand: King James I believed in demons. Fairy tales have a tangled relation to this history, for the stories develop within a complex of fancies, supersti-tions, and stories around supernatural creatures such as elves or jinn, but they also, over a long and varied development, express a way of discounting the terrors attached. It is now implicit in the term fairy tale that the story told is not credible, that it does not command serious allegiance or faith. Fairy tales in this way face two ways: towards a past realm of belief on one side and towards a sceptical present on the other. They offer the pleasures of imaginative entry into a world that does not have intellectual or religious authority. In that essay 'On Fairy-Stories', Tolkien remembers how he 'desired dragons with a profound desire'. He feels this desire, he continues, because 'The dragon had the trademark of Faerie written plain upon him. In whatever world he had his being it was an Other-world. Fantasy, the making or glimpsing of Otherworlds, was the heart of the desire of Faërie.' The Other Worlds which fairy tales explore open a way for writers and storytellers to speak in Other terms, especially when the native inhabitants of the imaginary places do not belong to an established living faith and therefore do not command belief or repudiation. The tongue can be very free when it is speaking outside the jurisdiction of religion.

Baba Yaga the ogress rides in a flying mortar and pestle (Figure 1), and uses the skulls of her victims for lamps on the fence of her forest lair, while her myopic German cousin in 'Hansel and Gretel' builds her house of gingerbread; French *fées* and Italian *fate* are beautiful, tall and stately, closer to the great ladies and enchanters who figure in the stories than to the wee folk—the imps, hobgoblins, and pixies who troop by twilight in the Celtic tradition. Different cultures produce different imaginary features for the population of fairytale settings: the genies of the *Arabian Nights* are smoky, fiery,

Figure 1 Baba Yaga rides through the forest in her mortar searching for prey, in *Vasilissa the Beautiful*, illustrated by Ivan I. Bilibin, 1902.

volatile, and infinitely shifting in size, sometimes gnarled and fearsome, sometimes graceful and incomparably beautiful; as they have Qur'anic authority and are part of orthodox Muslim cosmology, the stories read differently in their own homelands (see Figure 4).

Fairies do not need to appear to stamp a story a fairy tale: standard favourites ('Red Riding Hood', 'Puss-in-Boots', 'Rapunzel') do not feature them; new-fangled stories, which were thought of as fairy tales by their creators and first audiences, such as the *Alice* books, C. S. Lewis's Narnia cycle, and even 'Ali Baba and the Forty Thieves', do not include fairies as the agents of the wonders they relate. Magic, however, needs to be implied and present in a fairy tale, and it conjures the presence of another world, a sense that the story has casements thrown open on a view of fairyland, or, as John Keats spelled the word, on the realms of faery. The poet W. H. Auden, discussing these imaginary zones, adopted the term 'Secondary World', which had been used by Tolkien and C. S. Lewis, and declared, 'Every normal human being is interested in two kinds of worlds: the Primary, everyday, world which he knows through his senses, and a Secondary world or worlds which he not only can create in his imagination, but also cannot stop himself creating...Stories about the Primary world may be called Feigned Histories; stories about a Secondary world myths or fairy tales.' Secondary worlds can be mischievous and merry, as in Shakespeare's enchanted wood of *A Midsummer Night's Dream*, Christina Rossetti's luscious, sinister goblin orchards, the distant sumptuous Isles of the King of the Blue Jinn, or the chilly 'under-land of Null' evoked by the Scottish balladeer and poet Helen Adam; but whatever their atmosphere, they're also laboratories for experiments with thought, allegories of alternatives to the world we know. In the story 'Starlight' the French wit and social critic Henriette-Julie de Murat imagined a topsy-turvy world in which men rock the babies and women manage the peaceful nation. Lewis Carroll's Wonderland, John Ruskin's Stiria and its Golden River are also secondary worlds that refract our own, and are populated by imaginary alter egos, dream selves, and saviour figures, often a child quester, who face ordeals and enemies within and without. These fantastic horizons are fraught with the unknown or the intimated—the violence of monsters and the caprices of imps—or open to blissful idleness and pleasure (which present their own risks, of course), but they are by definition operating along mysterious lines, organized according to principles that differ from ordinary life. Fairylands are zones of enchantment; like the key in Bluebeard, they are *'fée'*, magic—as in 'fey', from 'fated', itself derived from *'fatum'*, meaning 'that which has been spoken'.

Dangers & Pleasures: Shape-Shifters, Doubles, and Goblin Men

The inhabitants of this other place, this enchanted dimension, play a part in the English Renaissance, and signalled the recovery of a native image store, beyond the classical tradition. Queen Mab is the fairies' midwife, as Mercutio tells Romeo in Shakespeare's play, and drives about in a chariot made from an empty hazel nut, harnessed by spiders' webs to 'a team of little atomies':

> And in this state she gallops night by night
> Through lovers' brains, and then they dream of love.

> (I.iv.70–1)

Queen Mab embodies three salient features of the fairy realm, which make it the necessary backdrop to the fairy tale as a story: her occupation involves her in secret intimacies, her closeness to dreams intensifies the powerful undercurrents of romance and eros in the genre, and her miniaturized universe draws attention to the unpredictable disjunctions of scale in the scenery of a fairy tale (the stories can include giants of colossal proportions alongside tiny pixies and sprites skipping daintily about to hang 'fairy favours' and dewdrops on cowslips' petals).

Puck is 'a Fairy' and 'a merry wanderer of the night', who boasts he can change himself into 'a filly foal' or 'a roasted crab'; Ariel in *The Tempest* is sometimes also called 'a Fairy', as well as an 'airy spirit' and a 'chick', and he shape-shifts—now a harpy, now a sea nymph, now a creature so small that he sings:

> Where the bee sucks, there suck I
> In a cowslip's bell I lie . . .

> (V.i.88–9)

He/she can also put 'a girdle around the earth in forty minutes', fly like a jinni, raise storms, and sing eerily of mysteries far beyond ordinary ken (see Figure 2).

But Ariel, a magical intermediate being who, while subject to Prospero's enchantments, is not subject to human laws, puts before us a new dimension of experience. Harold Bloom proposes that we grasp the function of Ariel and

Puck in rhetorical terms: they create a bridge between our human world and fairy worlds, conforming to what is known in George Puttenham's work *The Art of English Poesie* (1589) as a 'farfet', 'as when we had rather fetch a word a great way off then to use one nerer hand to expresse the matter as wel and plainer'. Ariel's presence does not make *The Tempest* a fairy tale, but it does reveal the form's connection to imaginative flights.

The learned élite became crucial to the collection of popular lore about fairies, long before the word 'folk-lore' was first used in English in 1846. In the seventeenth and eighteenth centuries in France, the craze for fairy tales, which took hold after the 1690s when Marie-Jeanne L'Héritier and Charles Perrault (an older relative of hers) began writing them, was intertwined with a rejection of classical myth, and ethnographical curiosity about the French and their true identity. In England, a combination of religious confusion and Enlightenment insatiability spurred divines and scholars to find out what ordinary people believed, and antiquarians such as Francis Douce and William Stukeley swelled the corpus of fairy lore, while in Scotland a similar impulse towards excavating a national past inspired the Reverend Robert Kirk to draw up an anthology of his parishioners' ideas about changelings, doppelgängers, fairy abductions, and what he calls 'Second Sight'. When the industrious folklorist Andrew Lang edited Kirk's manuscript in 1893, he gave it a new title, *The Secret Commonwealth of Fairies, Fauns and Elves*.

In these early modern fairylands we meet many returning magical motifs of fairy tales: uncanny powers of clairvoyance (second sight), abductions, spellbound sleep, doubles, curses, prophecies, and powerful charmed things. The straight, near scientific language of the ethnographer reporting from the field gives Kirk's work an enhanced strangeness: there is nothing like belief in the reality of something you think unreal to sharpen a sense of mystery and wonder. Such material nourishes the marrow of fairy tales: changelings, for example, range from the Indian boy in *A Midsummer Night's Dream* to the baleful baby made of ice in Maurice Sendak's most shivery picture book, *Outside Over There* (1981); the binding power of naming governs the plot of Rumpelstiltskin when the princess tricks him out of marrying her; doppelgängers inspire alarm and even madness in a story such as Hans Andersen's *The Shadow*; abduction into another enchanted world is a fundamental ordeal, poetically dramatized in Angela Carter's 'The Erl-King'.

When the Romantics were following up antiquarians' discoveries, they revived the fairies whom they encountered in ballads, nursery songs, local legends, and superstitions. Potent tales were scattered among these materials: Thomas Percy's *Reliques of Ancient Poetry* includes several traditional episodes about eerie enchantment, robber bridegrooms, and supernatural revenges for cruel death. Such marvellous and ancient stories jolt us out of the ordinary through the taste they give of the dangers—and the pleasures—of the fairy world.

In 1798, Wordsworth and Coleridge published the founding anthology of English Romanticism, *Lyrical Ballads*, in which Coleridge included several uncanny poems of the supernatural which have become touchstones of literary imagination:

Figure 2 The fairies dance their ringlets to the whistling wind. William Blake, *Oberon, Titania and Puck with Fairies Dancing, c.1786.*

the ballad of the Ancient Mariner and his accursed voyage, the tale of the spellbound, love-struck Christabel. In 1801, a friend of Coleridge's, the radical poet John Thelwall, wrote a long narrative poem embroidering on Arthurian themes, called *The Fairy of the Lake: A Dramatic Romance*; it features a sorceress as well as the benevolent heroine, her 'train of fairies', 'Giants of Frost', and 'Incubus, a frozen demon'. A few years later (1813) Percy Bysshe Shelley crossed Shakespeare's fairy midwife Queen Mab with the Queen of the Fairies, Titania, to conjure an ethereal vision in his long political poem called 'Queen Mab'. For these writers, Romantic fairies are the imagination's powerful voices, and

BOX 1   *Meeting the Fairy Queen*

In the mid-thirteenth century, a poet called Thomas of Erceldoune fell asleep on a bank on a steep hillside when a lady appeared to him: she was so beautiful he mistook her for the Virgin Mary, even though she was riding a horse caparisoned with silver bells and saddled with gold and ivory, and carrying a bow and arrows with three bloodhounds following and three greyhounds leashed. When he starts paying due homage to her magnificence, she rebuffs him; but he presses his suit. She warns that if she takes him with her, he'll have to become her slave—and at this point she turns into a hideous, palsied, leprous hag. But it is too late; he has surrendered himself into her hands. They start descending through the gathering gloom, past a roaring ocean and across rivers of blood; once through these horrors, they reach a smiling orchard where four paths meet. There, the Fairy Queen—for it is she of course—reveals herself in all her beauty and radiance and irresistibility, and tells Thomas where the paths lead: Heaven, Purgatory, Hell, and, the last, to Elfland. There, Thomas will stay with her, after she has laid him under a spell of silence for seven years.

At the end of this time, the Fairy Queen releases him. He believes he has only been gone seven days, and she sets him back on his way home with a great gift: once cursed with muteness, he'll now always speak true. He becomes 'Thomas the Rhymer', the first English-language poet in the literature, a writer who combines the roles of fantastic storyteller and seer. And of course one of the stories he tells is about his sojourn in the other world, one of the many underworlds that lie on the other side of reality.

When John Keats wrote 'La Belle Dame sans Merci' his head was filled with memories of such adventures in his poetic forerunners' lives.

> I met a lady in the meads,
>   Full beautiful—a faery's child,
> Her hair was long, her foot was light,
>   And her eyes were wild.
>
>   .   .   .   .
>
> She found me roots of relish sweet,
>   And honey wild, and manna-dew,
> And sure in language strange she said—
>   'I love thee true'.
>
> She took me to her elfin grot,
>   And there she wept and sighed full sore,
> And there I shut her wild wild eyes
>   With kisses four.

they can speak of 'unheard' things that cannot be spoken of in other ways openly. Coleridge's 'Christabel' stages a drama of high octane love between women, and enigmatic eroticism charges the dream of Keats's knight in his ballad, 'La Belle Dame sans Merci'.

The Victorians surpassed the enthusiasm of the Romantics in their pursuit of faerie lore, with Sir Walter Scott in Scotland brilliantly mining the stories he found from every source, oral and written, either at home in the Highlands or farther afield. Scott was a cultural patriot but also a synthesizer and omnivore on a Shakespearean scale. It was Scott who first brought Kirk's work on fairies to public notice, and in his *Letters on Demonology and Witchcraft* (1830), he passes on the marvellous legend of Thomas the Rhymer, who was snatched into a fairy hill by a Fairy Queen. This tale stages a classic encounter with the seductions of fairyland.

Storytelling is a dangerous vocation, for the fairies punish those who return to tell their secrets. The seventeenth-century poet Richard Corbet warns in 'Farewell, Rewards and Fairies': 'A tell-tale in their company | They never could endure!' Robert Kirk himself was stolen into a fairy hill one moonlit night, Walter Scott also reports, and was never seen again, punished for giving away secrets of the fairy commonwealth.

As Christina Rossetti dramatizes thrillingly in 'Goblin Market' (1862), her long, strange, narrative poem, creatures from fairyland may appear and capture you with their queer irresistible gifts:

> 'We must not look at goblin men,
> We must not buy their fruits...'

Her goblins are closer to Shakespeare's ambiguous fairies, Moth, Mustardseed, and Peaseblossom, than to that 'airy spirit' Ariel, and they're also given Bosch-like features, monstrous and metamorphic, furry and whiskered:

> Curious Laura chose to linger
> Wondering at each merchant man.
> One had a cat's face,
> One whisked a tail,
> One tramped at a rat's pace,
> One crawled like a snail,
>
> . . . .

> She heard a voice like voice of doves
> Cooing all together:
> They sounded kind and full of loves
> In the pleasant weather.

Laura gives a lock of her golden hair in exchange for the fruits the goblins are proffering; her sister Lizzie then has to place herself in grave danger, and wrestle with the 'queer little goblin men', in order to bring Laura back from the dead. In many ways, the sisters double each other. The scholar of Victorian literature, Isobel Armstrong, has commented, 'this is the most dazzling of the era's fairy creations . . . riddle-like poems of desire, exclusion and painful lack—poems structured through subtle negative particles and subjunctives which disclose haunting hypothetical worlds.' The state of sexual enthrallment that Rossetti conjures (Laura 'Sucking . . . sucked until her lips were sore . . .') transmutes into keyed-up fairy imagery and hypnotic lullaby the poet's experience of young women's ordeals, for Rossetti herself worked with unmarried mothers in Highgate penitentiary near her house and, like her friend Lewis Carroll, campaigned against the exploitation of children.

The poem is a characteristic story of faerie, an original invention inspired by folklore about fairy abductions. It is a brilliant, perturbing, invented fairy tale in verse which springs from principles laid down in the folkloric tradition about a possible other world nearby.

Christina Rossetti was also one of the Victorian writers who identified children as a special readership for fairy tale and related material, and in *Sing Song* (1879–93) she adopted the patter of nursery rhymes in charm-like verses:

> 'Kookoorookoo! kookoorookoo!'
> Crows the cock before the morn;
> 'Kikirikee! kikirikee!'
> Roses in the east are born.
> 'Kookoorookoo! kookoorookoo!'
> Early birds begin their singing;
> 'Kikirikee! kikirikee!'
> The day, the day, the day is springing.

Folklore, Patriots, and Localism

Although fairies were already beginning to decline into sentimental whimsy, they were still powerful beings in the imagination of the Irish poet W. B. Yeats, who wrote to regain the lost time of Celtic faerie, and, alongside his friends Speranza Wilde (Oscar's mother) and his closest ally and associate Augusta, Lady Gregory, became the catalyst of the Celtic twilight's resurrection of Irish folk tales. They collected them to uncover 'the singularity of the nation'. Regarding the wee folk, Yeats made common cause with the Scots and the Irish against the English, declaring that 'the world is... more full of significance to the Irish peasant than to the English. The fairy populace of hill and lake and woodland have helped to keep it so.' For Yeats, fairyland ensured poetry. He quotes a Gaelic proverb as an example of the vitality of mind and language that he prized, which he connected implicitly to faery lore: 'The lake is not burdened by its swan, the steed by its bridle, or a man by the soul that is in him.'

What did Scott, Rossetti, Keats, or Coleridge really think about the fairies they evoke in word and image? Few would argue that they believed in them, but they attributed belief to others. This form of surrogacy, which transposes belief on to another, occurs frequently in the history of fantasy, and many writers at different times have engaged passionately by proxy in the fairy world. Most of the accounts of encounters in fairyland report incidents and adventures that occurred to someone else. This is the terrain of anecdote, ghost sightings, and old wives' tales, of oral tradition, hearsay, superstition, and shaggy dog stories: once upon a time and far away among another people ...

The greatest writers about other worlds—from Shakespeare to Rossetti to Yeats—summon up Queen Mab and Robin Goodfellow and Puck in all their peculiar detail, and they woo their audiences to surrender to 'antique fables and fairy toys'. But they bend the material through dream frames that distance it from immediate testimony. Like medieval kings who kept a ragged and filthy hermit at court to pray on their behalf, we—sceptical, worldly dwellers in culture's mindscapes—need proxies to prevent the deforestation and depopulating of fancy's traditional territory. J. M. Barrie dramatized this manoeuvre of belief-by-proxy in *Peter Pan*, in the famous scene when the fairy Tinkerbell drinks poison and Peter turns to the audience and tells us to clap our hands to save her. In the book of the play, published later, Barrie wrote,

> The fairies are nearly all dead now ... where the first baby laughed for the first time, the laugh broke into a thousand

pieces and they all went skipping about, and that was the beginning of fairies. And now when every new baby is born its first laugh becomes a fairy... Children know such a lot now. Soon they don't believe in fairies, and every time a child says, 'I don't believe in fairies' there is a fairy somewhere that falls down dead.

This emotional blackmail—with its shameless pulling of the heartstrings—remains fractured by the irony that however loud we clap to show our faith, Barrie isn't sincere and neither are we, and if the children with us are convinced, they're the dupes of a need that adults feel, which children meet.

By 1906, when Rudyard Kipling wrote *Puck of Pook's Hill* in defence of the ancient lost fairy world of Britain, the fairies had been successfully prettified; he railed against 'little buzz-flies with butterfly wings and gauze petticoats and shiny stars in their hair and a wand... painty-winged wand-waving sugar-and-shake-your-head set of impostors...'.

The nexus of fantasy, nationalist antiquarianism, and romantic longings for an imaginary innocent past, a child-hood of the tribe, continued to find in fairyland's denizens its ideal representatives. In Britain, Tolkien's scholarly inter-ests led to his triumphant invention of the Shire, the other world of the Hobbits—they are rather late incomers in the census of fairyland, but they grow out of the professor's deep knowledge of Anglo-Saxon and Celtic myth and narrative; in *The Lord of the Rings*, he reinvigorated and transmuted figures and creatures he had found in epic and romance and deployed them through Middle Earth. Other imaginary worlds occupy magical kingdoms under the sea, castles deep in the enchanted forest, or fairy hills; they are found at 'The Back of the North Wind', in Elfland, Wonderland, Neverland, Narnia, or 'East of the Sun and West of the Moon', as in the title of the Norwegian fairy tale about a girl who quests far and wide through thick and thin for her lost beloved bear.

The activities of a folklore scholar like Katharine Briggs, who compiled her fantastic *Dictionary of the Fairies*, and of Jorge Luis Borges, who created a wonderfully entertaining treasury, called *The Book of Imaginary Beings* (which includes beasts and monsters 'imagined' by Kafka, C. S. Lewis, et al.), spurred on, in turn, the imagination of later generations to populate these secondary worlds. Rare bogles and boggarts and grylli whom scholars had unearthed began to colonize new, popular narratives: the role-playing games of *Dungeons and Dragons*, and J. K. Rowling's Harry Potter series teem with once endangered species of fairy folk. Fairyland undergoes constant re-stocking and re-invention. As the home territory of fantasy, it attracts new settlers, monsters and marvels, their species increased by widening encounters with cultures beyond Europe on the one hand, and by the expanding potential of computer-generated imagery (CGI) on the other (Gollum, a splendid concoction of Tolkien's, was unforgettably realized by new techniques in the films of the books). These games and successful fictions are not fairy tales as such, but draw on their legacy. While 'here be dragons' might announce a land of marvels, the words do not ipso facto turn the story in which they appear into a fairy tale. But enchanted territories and their fantasy population are the givens of fairy stories, even when these narrative features are not explicitly present or active. The premise of a Secondary World beyond this one acts like the live culture necessary to turn milk into yoghurt, or the 'mother' that transforms wine into vinegar.

The powerful underlying motives for the construction of these untrue stories include a need to move beyond the limits of reality. Once there, many consequences follow, but one of the main effects is speculative pleasure. 'There is more bliss in describing the nymphs than in describing medals,' declared Paracelsus. 'There is more bliss in describing the origin of the giants than in describing court etiquettes. There is more bliss in describing Mélusine than in describing cavalry and artillery. There is more bliss in describing the mountain people underground than in describing fencing and service to ladies.'

Or, to put it in fairytale terms, there is more magic in inaugurating a different reality, to meet the hunger of hope and desire.

2

With a Touch of Her Wand

Magic & Metamorphosis

In a true fairy tale everything must be wondrous—mysterious and unconnected—everything animated.

Novalis

'What is Real?' asked the Rabbit one day . . .
'Real isn't how you are made,' said the Skin Horse. 'It's a thing that happens to you. When a child loves you for a long, long time, not just to play with, but REALLY loves you, then you become real?' . . .
'Does it hurt?' asked the Skin Rabbit.
'Sometimes,' said the Skin Horse . . .

Margery Williams, *The Velveteen Rabbit*

'Magic tale' has also been suggested as a term that captures the idea of the form better than 'fairy tale' or even 'wonder tale'; it points to the pivotal role that enchantment plays, both in the action of the stories and the character of its agents. Such stories assume that visible and invisible beings intercommunicate and they present this state as if it were immemorial, the default condition of the mythic imagination; the tales take place in an animist landscape, in which everything is animated—animals speak, stones move of their own accord. Enchantment, however, has its own changing history, its own tides and currents, from medieval faerie to Romantic possession and hauntedness, from sceptical magic entertainment to the contemporary technological uncanny.

Classic fairy tales, deploying wonders and inspiring astonishment, depend on magic as causation; magic is part of the fabric of everyday reality, which is permeated with invisible forces moved by magical beings, who mostly act beyond the protagonists' reach and spring continual surprises, behave capriciously, and create unforeseeable effects which contradict the laws of physics, logic, and probability. The gold and glass, forests and animals, all vividly and physically embodied, reach out to the listener and the reader and pull us in to the story, and there everything changes, for the laws of nature are disregarded and the plots work instead according to the laws of enchantment. Glass is used for shoes; also for mountains; in the form of a mirror, it speaks, or in the form of a distaff it shatters when its maiden owner sleeps with a roving rogue. Characters in fairy tales have magical powers—for better or worse. The world does not operate as we know it: time and space shrink and stretch. Aurora sleeps for a hundred years and wakes up young (though the palace chef, when ordered to cook her, is worried she might have become a bit tough); Tom Thumb survives a dozen misadventures against adversaries the size of volcanoes. Seven-league boots and cloaks of invisibility offer protection—or, in the wrong hands, threats.

The Magic of Nature

Animals speak, especially birds, and no one in a fairy tale is taken aback when rocks and trees and streams and waterfalls act under their own volition or shape-shift from one form to another (see Figure 3); protagonists take it in their stride that if you drink the water of a certain stream, you will be turned into a wolf or a deer or a dragon or a snake. In order to survive, heroes and heroines rely on beasts (see Figure 10) or use their wits: sometimes by prising out the evildoers' secrets. The dead cannot be suppressed; animate forces keep circulating regardless of individual bodies and their misadventures. Even when a tree has been cut down and turned into a table or a spindle, its wood is still alive with the currents of power that charge the forest where it came from. The singing bone of the murder victim in a traditional ballad denounces his or her killers; in the story of 'The Greek King and Doctor Douban' from the *Arabian Nights*, the doctor's severed head speaks after death, and, with thrilling inexorableness, inflicts death by poison on the tyrant who murdered him. Revenge, served cold. Aschenputtel, the Grimms' Cinderella, in the tale written over a hundred years after Perrault's classic 'Cendrillon', plants a twig on the grave of her mother, and it grows into a hazel tree; when she grieves there, and cries because she's been forbidden to go to the ball, the tree shakes down a golden dress and golden shoes for her to wear. This happens three times. No wand, no pumpkin,

Figure 3 Living nature: every tree may be friend...or foe. 'Little Brother and Little Sister' by the Brothers Grimm, illustrated by Arthur Rackham, 1917.

or rat, or lizard, no fairies. The spirit of Cinderella's dead mother flows through nature and sparks the tree, inspiring the birds to help her daughter, and later to peck out the eyes of her wicked stepsisters.

The emphasis on nature and phantoms is recognizably Romantic, and the modern fairy tale that evolved through the work of the Grimm Brothers and other collectors relies on an idea of natural magic. Magic in European fairy tale works along lines closer to magnetism and the pull of the tides or the silence of eclipse, because it reflects a vision of organic correspondences that developed in early modern society. It was in the fifteenth century, for example, that Paracelsus, the Swiss physician and alchemist, first classified elemental beings: he called them gnomes (earth), sylphs (air), salamanders (fire), and undines (water). Each was destined to spark the narrative imagination to such an extent they now appear generic fairytale characters.

These supernatural creatures entered our thinking about the population of faerie from German culture: Goethe dramatized the Paracelsian vision in his vast poetic drama *Faust*, and the artist Phillip Otto Runge, who set down on paper for the first time the extraordinary, powerful story of 'The Juniper Tree', painted many scenes of fairyland, its spirits and changelings, bathed in a golden otherworldly light. The English poets, especially Coleridge, were profoundly influenced by this predominantly German dream of a pastoral uncanny, and Romantic writers everywhere enriched it. Another fatal romance, for example, overtakes a mortal when the water nymph Undine emerges from a spring in

Friedrich de La Motte Fouqué's elaborate Romantic fairy tale of *c*.1811; she then migrates through literature and ballet and eventually takes her place among Disney princess dolls as red-haired, fish-tailed Ariel, the Little Mermaid. The magical motifs in the vision of the mystically minded German Romantic poet Novalis shed all folkloric and religious baggage to become symbolic ciphers enclosing secret wisdom: he yearned to discover the blue flower, his holy grail. In the work of such idealists, fairy tale turns into metaphysical allegory. Goethe's story, simply entitled 'A Fairy Tale', reads woodenly for contemporary readers, but the librettist of Mozart's *The Magic Flute*, and Hugo von Hofmannstahl for Richard Strauss's opera *Die Frau ohne Schatten* (The Woman Without a Shadow) belong in this lineage, and their language of symbols is memorably peculiar and powerfully grounded in human passions.

Into the Woods

Those powers who govern the multiple currents of supernatural power are sometimes recognizable as dangerous, sometimes disguised as friendly, sometimes ambiguous. They can be seductive, they can tempt us with presents (gingerbread houses with windowpanes of sugar; juicy red apples), or draw us into a conspiracy of terror. Queens of the Night demand our obedience; ogres threaten; witches infest the woods. Inhabitants of fairylands often live apart from human society—in the depths of the forest, or in a far distant castle—but evil-doers also occupy the heart of the home: the wicked mother, the queen, and the fabled stepmother return again and again, in one story after another, as the agents of potent and lethal spells (see Figure 16). In 'The Prince of the Black Islands', the beautiful wife of the hero drugs him so she can visit her lover, and cruelly changes her husband half to stone and beats him. The wicked queen uses poison in 'Snow White'; Mother Gothel, the old witch, imprisons Rapunzel in a high tower with no door and cuts off her hair when she tries to escape. Sometimes the evil figure doesn't cast spells or work magic but acts against nature so profoundly that she exudes diabolical perversity, tantamount to black magic—when she abandons her children in the forest to die because the family has no food. Sometimes she has no motive, indeed seems to be acting against her own interests, so possessed by malice that she'd rather destroy herself than let anyone else flourish: in 'The Sleeping Beauty', she orders the palace chef to casserole her daughter-in-law and grandchildren.

Females dominate fairytale evil. However, ogres share witches' appetite and bloodthirstiness—they're a species from another alien world, but they are often slow-witted, bumbling giants not gifted at magic at all. Cheeky Jack gets the better of one, with the help of his kindly wife, in an English favourite, 'Jack and the Beanstalk'. Jack is a trickster figure, and widespread throughout European fairy tales and beyond. A trickster heroine like Finette, who avenges her sisters against their abductor, also overcomes the villainous ogre, when he is bent on seduction as in the Bluebeard group of stories about a serial murderer.

Enemies lurk in the woods and some beasts are wholly unregenerate, however: beware the wolf. He comes in disguise, and looks as sweet and gentle as Granny in bed in her bonnet. In raunchy traditional versions, Little Red Riding Hood isn't taken in by the wolf in Granny's bed. As Angela Carter puts it, she is 'nobody's meat'.

Yet nature also wraps the protagonist in intimate relationships, and many creatures are on our side, it turns out; they are gallant and faithful and resourceful. In the exuberant fairy tales of Marie-Catherine D'Aulnoy, wildernesses are forbidding, but they also harbour friends and familiars—the good little mouse, the loving great green worm (who is not requited). D'Aulnoy shows the influence of the *Arabian Nights*, in which animal metamorphoses are elaborate, involving numerous adventures, as in 'The Tale of the Second Dervish', in which the prince is turned into a monkey and performs many marvels on behalf of his rescuer. In 'Hansel and Gretel', a duck befriends the children and carries them back home safe and sound on her back. An ugly fish—a flounder—turns out to be as all-powerful as a god until the fisherman's wife asks for one wish too many. In 'The Juniper Tree', when the sister, little Marlene (Marleen, Marlinchen), buries her murdered brother's bones with his mother's beneath the tree 'it began to move. The branches separated and came together again as though they were clapping their hands in joy. At the same time smoke came out of the tree, and in the middle of the smoke there was a flame that seemed to be burning. Then a beautiful bird flew out of the fire and began singing magnificently.' This is her brother reborn, metamorphosed into a glorious phoenix, who works his revenge:

'It was my mother who butchered me,
It was my father who ate me,
My sister, little Marlene,
Found all my little bones,
Bound them in a silken cloth,
And laid them under the Juniper tree.
Peewit, peewit, what a beautiful bird am I!'

The story drives to its cruel end: 'As she [the wife/step-mother] went out the door, crash! The bird threw the mill-stone down on her head and she was crushed to death. The father and Marlene heard the crash and went outside. Smoke, flames, and fire were rising from the spot, and when it was over, the little brother was standing there. He took his father and Marlene by the hand, and all three were very happy. Then they went into the house, sat down at the table, and ate.'

With the bad mother destroyed, the family regroups around the paternal table—exonerating the father altogether from having guzzled on his dead son's flesh.

Not all powerful wielders of magic are irreversibly good or evil; this unpredictability adds to the dramatic effects of the fairy tale: jinn can be converted to virtue and act lavishly on behalf of the heroes and heroines, and a witch like Mother Holle, who when she shakes out her feather bedclothes makes snow fall on earth, can change the fortunes of a good kind girl but act very cruelly to a bad unkind sister.

The anthropologist Claude Lévi-Strauss famously commented that animals were 'bons à penser', good to think with, and fairy tales speak through beasts to explore common experiences—fear of sexual intimacy, assault, cruelty, and injustice and, in general, the struggle for survival. A tradition of articulate, anthropomorphized creatures of every kind is as old as literature itself: animal fables and beast fairy tales are found in ancient Egypt and Greece and India, and the legendary Aesop of the classics has his story-telling counterparts all over the world, who moralize crows and ants, lions and monkeys, jackals and foxes and donkeys, to mock the follies and vices of human beings and display along the way the effervescent cunning and high spirits of the fairytale genre.

By contrast with animal fables, where something of an animal's observable, actual character helps make the point (monkeys are clever, sharks, well, shark-like, in 'The Heart of a Monkey' from Zanzibar), the beast of fairytale romance comes in fantasy shape—mythological creatures such as a dragon, a snake, a yellow dwarf, or the 'Great Green Worm' (A. S. Byatt's rendering of D'Aulnoy's 'Le Serpentin vert'), and they belong in a world of romance and psychology rather than satire and practical wisdom. Monster bride-grooms can also take the form of animals that used to pose a very real threat—wolves and bears and pigs and warthogs (Walter Crane's chosen beast for his elaborate and richly coloured illustrations of 'Beauty and the Beast'). Mme de Murat even imagined an unwanted husband in the shape of a rhinoceros—then a novelty in Europe. Often hybrid, huge, scaly, tusked, and bristling, such beasts endanger and even rape the heroine, in far-flung exotic settings or close to home. Protagonists mutate into a strange, often loathsome and sometimes terrifying outward shape, a boar, a bear, a snake, or a raven, often the outer proof of their inner viciousness. Angela Carter chose to translate 'Prince Chéri', another of D'Aulnoy's tales, in which the good Fairy Candida changes Prince Sweetheart into a monster: 'Henceforward, you shall look like what you are—angry as a lion, brutal as a bull, greedy as a wolf, and treacherous as a snake.' But the victims of metamorphosis can also be innocent, and assume a more domestic, hapless, absurd animal form—an ass, a ram, a frog, a bird, a hedgehog.

No power of witches or gnomes or goblins or ogres or beasts, however, can completely extinguish the intrinsic good of the life force that runs through nature. The vital current enlivens everything, no matter how inert. It doesn't depend on being housed in individuals or their bodies, but like a lizard that grows another tail when one has been cut off, a fairytale victim can hardly ever be extinguished.

Charmed Life, Active Things

The vehicle of magical effects does not however need to have possessed life in the first place: *inorganic* things are also animate and dynamic. While magical life forces flow principally through natural phenomena—flora, fauna, bodies—ordinary things can become spellbound as well as spellbinding; they can be charmed and changed by the right combination of words, which is usually a secret only the witch or the magician or the clever animal helper knows, but which the protagonists sometimes overhear and can use as well. The wise women who come to the christening feast of the baby princess, Briar Rose, heap presents on her, but one of the wise women isn't given a gold plate to eat off, and she curses her: 'In her fifteenth year, the princess shall prick herself with a spindle and fall down dead!' Another wise woman—sometimes the youngest fairy present—reprieves the little victim, and though she is not strong enough to lift the curse altogether, Briar Rose instead 'shall fall into a deep sleep for one hundred years...'.

The king and queen give the order that every spindle be destroyed. But the princess later climbs a tower in the castle and finds there an old woman spinning—and the fatal words come true.

Spells are principally verbal: 'Open Sesame!', 'Rapunzel, Rapunzel, Let down your hair!' The dynamics of the narrative assume their efficacy: nobody in a fairy tale scoffs at a curse or prophecy or dire prohibition.

Animist vitality endows inert objects with active power (Princess Badoura's talisman and Aladdin's lamp in the *Nights*, Bluebeard's bloody key, Cinderella's glass slipper); the plots are carried forward by self-moving objects often in combination with the right formulae (the flying carpet, the magic club that attacks all comers, the magic tablecloth that always spreads a feast, the magic mirror, in 'Snow White', which tells the wicked queen the truth). Alongside the powerful enchanters, cannibal witches and ogres, elves, gnomes, nixies or water sprites, the speaking 'poetical animals', fairytale magic works through the uncanny activity of these inert objects, and it deepens the sense that invisible powers exist around us, and intensifies the thrill, the strangeness and terror of the pervasive atmosphere of enchantment. Magical worlds are a danger zone.

Fairy tales operate according to several other fundamental principles of magical thinking besides natural magic and animist vitality: animal metamorphosis and changeable bodies on the one hand, and the binding power of promises and curses on the other, govern the logic of the plots— although logic is hardly the *mot juste*, since magic springs continual surprises that break all the rules of probability. The implied, ever-present possibility of transmogrification means that fairytale protagonists, like the orphan and his sister in 'The Juniper Tree', a feckless hero like Aladdin, and a virtuous heroine like Petrosinella (an Italian Rapunzel), may be changed, sometimes literally, sometimes figuratively. A stroke of fate will raise them high or lay them low. We readers are placed on their side and we feel keenly the danger of falling under a spell, condemned to die at the hands of a cruel stepmother or a witch with little near-sighted red eyes.

Although magic operates according to fundamental principles, its manifestations differ from culture to culture, and era to era, which adds spice and variety to fairy tales. In the classic French 'Cinderella', Charles Perrault's *Cendrillon, ou le petit pantoufle de verre*, the fairy godmother conjures the slippers and the dress and the pumpkin coach and the rat coachman and the lizard footmen, and Perrault, ever the worldly courtier, stresses at the end in his *moralité* that it's crucial for everyone to have such a figure in their lives—a society patron. The fairy godmother is the principal agent of the transformations that take place, and he shifts the origin of her powers from supernatural to social: from gods to patricians.

In versions collected in other cultures, Cinderella's dead mother returns in the form of an animal, who cares for her and feeds her: a little cow in the Scottish tale 'Rashen Coatie', a cat in Angela Carter. The enchantments in the *Arabian Nights* work within a cosmology of daemonic energy, flowing through

Figure 4 Jinn: unpredictable, metamorphic, hybrid beings with immense magical powers can be male (as here) or female. Tile inspired by *Marvels of Things Created and Miraculous Aspects of Things Existing* by al-Qazwini, Iran, 19th century.

the jinn, who are somewhat like fairies, intermediate beings between angels and humans (Figure 4). In 'The Tale of the Fisherman and the Genie', the genie Sakhr streams out of an old barnacled copper flask fished up from the depths of the sea; he has been shut up inside with a stopper of lead stamped with the seal of Solomon, but when a fisherman opens it and releases him, he towers to the sky, his powers to do good or ill undiminished by his long inactivity inside the bottle. This is the elemental landscape of wonder, humming with invisible forces and other-than-human creatures.

The Magic of Metamorphosis

The way magic runs against the grain of reality, making all these improbable twists and turns, lifts the tale into the realm of surprise. Or rather, into the realm of surprisingness, as C. S. Lewis realized, because we have heard the story before and we know what will happen. Even if we cannot remember it exactly, we expect the ending to be happy because this is a fairy tale. Cinderella will be recognized for her true self; Snow White will be jolted on her bier and cough up the piece of apple that's choking her; the evil stepmother will meet her doom—and this foreknowledge increases rather than decreases our sense of satisfaction at the happy outcome.

Walter Benjamin, who in 1936 wrote a marvellous essay called 'The Storyteller', likes the justice meted out in the tales by magic. He comments that they give hope that 'cunning and high spirits' will win in the end against dark malignant forces.

33

Metamorphosis in fairy tales has a clear relation with myth, and fairytale variants spin twists on the tradition: for example, the 'witch's duels', or battle sequences of ever-changing metamorphoses as one character battles with another, pick up the struggle of shape-shifters like Thetis against Peleus's advances, but whereas in myths the outcome is not happy (shape-shifting Thetis is overborne by Peleus, and conceives Achilles), such battles in fairy tale end with the defeat of the enemy or the happy triumph of the hero (see Figure 11). The price can be high: the apocalyptic contest between a princess and the evil jinni in the Second Dervish's Tale ends with his destruction, but she is scorched by her own fiery metamorphoses, and cannot survive. It is a sign of the trend in early twentieth-century fairy tale that when Lotte Reiniger adapted the scene in her 1926 film, *The Adventures of Prince Achmed*, the 'Witch of the Fire Mountain' prevails against the Demons of Waq Waq. During the course of a furious shape-shifting duel, her adversaries morph from lion to scorpion to serpent, to eagle, to cat, cock, etc. and maul and pounce and grapple, flowing apparently seamlessly from one form to another. This sequence, the first of its kind on screen, exploits the extraordinary potential film animation offers for fluid metamorphosis in movement and has had a significant influence: on the wizards' duel in *The Sword and the Stone*, for example (Disney, 1963).

The enchanters and enchantresses of fairy tales (Figure 5) also have recognizable mythic counterparts. Circe, who changes men into beasts in both Homer and in Ovid, and her niece, Medea, are the precursors of many fascinating sorceresses, such as the Queen of the Serpents in the prodigious sequence of fairy tales about the hero Buluqiya in the

Figure 5 The wicked wizard wears a crocodile skin and brandishes a wand of writhing serpents in 'The Golden Branch' by Marie-Catherine D'Aulnoy, illustrated by Clinton Peters, 1900.

35

Arabian Nights, or the many evil queens and stepmothers, who are equally skilled at poisons and potions and trans-mogrifying their victims: they can make a donkey's tail grow from the brow of an unkind sister, or another spit toads and snakes when she speaks; Joringel is changed into a bird and kept in a cage until Jorinda rescues him; the wicked queen in 'Snow White' turns herself into an old pedlar and offers her victim a poisoned comb, stay-laces, and, finally, the apple.

Unlike classical myths, fairy tales usually restore the victims of metamorphosis to their original form. Or they trans-figure them to be far more beautiful than before. The restoration leads to recognition: when the beast guise falls away, the true prince appears. In every case, the outer form has hidden the inner man, and it takes something momentous to overturn the beast's fate. Beast fairy tales like these follow a narrative arc: the story begins with a spell or a curse that binds the male hero under a terrible disguise, and after a passage of ordeals and horrors, closes with recognition and fulfilment (these are Cinderella tales with a male protagonist). Sometimes the plot follows emotional or psychological logic, but not always; a great deal of the impact of these fairy tales depends on the stark absence of explanation, on the sheer mysteriousness of the premises and outcome: how did the Beast come to be a Beast? Why is Hans a hedgehog? The stories are moulded to traditional patterns which lead our expectations as listeners or readers, but getting to the dénouement goes by unpredictable and wayward routes: burning the snakeskin, in Basile's tale 'Il re serpente' (The Snake King), or hurling the frog against the wall of the princess's bedroom in 'The Frog Prince'.

BOX 2 *Animal Metamorphosis: The Silence of the Deer*
....

In the Grimms' 'Little Brother and Little Sister', the evil step-mother, who 'can see through her eyelids' (Philip Pullman), follows the children who have run away deep into the forest; she casts a spell on the forest streams—three times. Listening to the babbling water, Little Sister, like a far more heroic figure of legend, is able to decipher what it is saying, and as her brother cups his hands to drink, she cries out, 'Don't drink! The spring is bewitched. Anyone who drinks from it will become a tiger. Put it down, put it down! You'll tear me to pieces!'

At the next spring, she hears it warn that anyone who drinks there will turn into a wolf. Once more, Little Sister manages to curb her brother. But the third time, she is too late; he drinks, 'And at once his face changed, and lengthened, and became covered in fine hairs, and his limbs changed into a deer's legs and he stood up, tottering uncertainly—and there he was, a young deer, a fawn.'

After this, as in an Ovidian metamorphosis, the deer can understand and feel with Little Brother's fully human con-sciousness, but he's beastlike in his instincts, is no longer able to speak, and rushes off to the sound of the hunters' horns.

This tender, poetic fairy tale reveals an underlying relation between human beings and all phenomena. These relations have no inherent ethical scaffolding; magic is arbitrary. The forest can shelter the children, or not. The springs can turn malevolent, and their powers are limited—they can warn potential victims, but have to obey the spell cast on them by a witch. Above all, the fairy tale assumes that Little Brother can turn into an animal. Nobody remarks on this, or on his change back into human form. It would not be a fairy tale from the Grimms' collection if anyone expressed surprise.

Occasionally, as in the magnificent group of fairy tales which Andersen revisits in 'The Wild Swans', the trace of the animal lingers—in the wing of one of the heroine's transformed brothers, because she has not had time to finish the shirt she has been so painfully weaving and sewing from star flowers or nettles. The scent—the miasma—of faery enchantment rises sharply from that unfinished sleeve, that remaining wing.

Heroines also suffer degrading disguise when they conceal their true identity under ashes and dirt, or shroud themselves in a wooden cloak, a coat of rushes, or the hide of a donkey or a bear. They aren't 'translated' into animal shape, like Bottom or the Frog King, but hidden, often at their own initiative in order to elude an unwanted lover—sometimes their own father, as in the fairy tale 'Peau-d'âne' (Donkeyskin). This incest plot was so widespread that, in Perrault's time, *un conte de peau d'âne* meant a fairy tale. The anthropologist James MacTaggart, when gathering material in the rural region of Estremadura, Spain, found that the heroine of their local variant of 'Donkeyskin' was wrapped in a pelican skin. He was puzzled (this is a part of the world where there have never been pelicans). But he soon discovered that goitre was endemic in the region, and realized that the imagery of the large bird with its baggy crop reflected the disfiguring swollen neck caused by malfunctioning of the thyroid gland, and that the familiar fairy tale was clothed in the specific conditions in that community.

Female protagonists are mutilated more often than male heroes, but this cruel variety of bodily transformation can be miraculously reversed, when their severed hand is found in a fish, or when their beaten and scarred bodies are healed by the good offices of the Sultan Haroun al-Rashid (with the help of a jinniya obedient to his commands) as in the cycle of 'The Porter and the Five Ladies of Baghdad' in the *Nights*. However, gender does not make such a difference when it comes to being devoured and regurgitated, whole. Magically, Red Riding Hood and Granny are cut out from the belly of the wolf, Tom Thumb survives being swallowed by an ogre, and the little boy victim in 'The Juniper Tree' reappears safe and sound.

A reversal of animal and other metamorphosis, leading to recognition of the protagonist's value and virtue, provides the determining structure of classic fairy tales. The best-known fairy tale in the popular group known as Beast Bridegroom tales is 'Beauty and the Beast', written by Jeanne-Marie Leprince de Beaumont, a governess working in England, and published in 1758 in *The Misses' Magazine*, a miscellany she put together to teach her charges. Beaumont adapted an earlier, intricate, protracted romance, 'La Belle et la bête' (1740) by Mme de Villeneuve, one of the *salonnières*. In Villeneuve's tale, the Beast has been cursed by his older godmother—after he rejected her advances (!). Beaumont reined in the rococo flourishes and corrected the morals: she swung the fairy tale more towards an ideal alliance, evoking a bourgeois romance designed to soothe young women facing arranged marriages; the tale invites them to accept the match their father proposes, however unappealing they find the prospective husband. They will come to love him, the story reassures them.

Beaumont's story has become a much-loved classic, much adapted, much performed, and it doesn't succeed in suppressing the erotic undertow that pulls so deeply in all these stories of beasts. When Jean Cocteau made his film of *La Belle et la bête* in 1946, he cast Jean Marais as the Beast, all aquiver with life: who can ever forget how he seems to catch fire when Belle rejects him and how his whole body smokes and his claws and pelt smoulder after he's made a kill, while he visibly grieves at these signs of his own monstrosity? Marais in his full hairy mask captures a perfect and irresistible synthesis of repulsiveness and attractiveness, and Cocteau's realization of a dream about the power of love has exercised its seduction for over half a century.

The Magic of Words

The stress falls on the binding power of words: the father must keep his promise to the Beast, the beauty will sleep for a hundred years, according to the letter of the spell. Readers and audiences grasp the importance of paying attention to what is said. These narrative elements are historic survivals from a pre-literate society when concepts of honour and trust provided the foundation for stability. The fairy tales themselves, growing out the spoken word, dramatizing fateful charms and spells, playing with meaning and double entendres, become part of that legislating fabric, and by issuing warnings about what happens to kings and princesses, wolves and other beasts who don't keep their promises, remind us to keep ours (see Figure 12).

Prophecies—and curses—march on unstoppably. One message of fairy tales is 'Beware what you wish for.' Another would be 'Beware what you promise.' Yet another would be 'Beware what you utter.' You can't take back what you say. There's a profound respect in the genre for what words do in the world, as well as in the stories. Of all the charged, active, enchanted elements in the tales, it is the words of the story that possess charmed life. Spells are formed of repetition, rhyme, and nonsense; when they occur in fairy tales, they're often in verse—riddles and ditties, and they belong to the same family of verbal patterning as counting out, skipping songs, and nursery rhymes.

The pleasure of these refrains arises from their absurdity, and they are often chanted over and over; patterning weaves the spell tighter, and repeating formulae thrice packs the power into the spell more strongly. Names are comical and mysterious in a memorable way: after Old Rinkrank has imprisoned the princess in a glass tower, he tells her she's now called Mother Mansrot. He calls out to her:

> 'It's me poor Old Rinkrank
> On my seventeen-foot legs
> On my one great swollen foot
> Mother Mansrot open the door.'

The mood can be shuddery comic:

> 'Fee fi fo fum
> I smell the blood of an Englishman
> Be he alive or be he dead
> I'll grind his bones to make my bread.'

Or uncanny and perverse, as in the English folk tale, 'The Three Heads in the Well': when each severed head rises spookily from the depths, it asks:

> 'Faire maiden, white and red
> Stroke me smoothe and combe my head...'

If its wish is met, it promises:

> 'And every haire a sheave shall be
> And every sheave a goulden tree.'

Such fragments of verse often survive from anonymous, undatable sources. For example, the patchwork of proverbs, saws, riddles, and allusions in the speech of Lear's Fool, of Edgar in disguise as Poor Tom, of mad Ophelia, has been pieced by Shakespeare from a ragbag of sources already anonymous and ancient—and often baffling—when he was writing. The web of words ensnares the cast of characters in the tale as surely as it intends to enthral us.

Patterns of repetition widen out from the brief rhymes and charms into whole structures of incident, with internal architecture reprising a similar episode again and again—most often in threes, but also in sixes and sevens, and in the *Arabian Nights* in thousands—multitudes of proliferating incidents, each with their own multitude of jinn. The numbers are dizzy-making, macro versions of the tiny incantations at the core of the plot's driving magical powers.

Magic, being a compact between practitioner and client, requires an audience for its accomplice; it depends on the consent of the participants, on 'that willing suspension of disbelief' Coleridge famously invoked on behalf of the supernatural in his poems. Rhyme, repetition, rhythmic prose or verse carry traces of oral performance and act as mnemonic markers. They also draw attention to the teller, who frequently opens and closes with a set phrase in order to frame as fairy tale what the audience is about to hear and help us enter the world where magical thinking rules. These verbal devices request the consent of the audience to accept what is to come, however unlikely. One could say, they cast a spell.

In this way, the storyteller adopts the devices of verbal magic; the animate forces ascribed to the world of phenomena by fairy tale as a genre are infused into the individual stories themselves.

3

Voices on the Page

Tales, Tellers, & Translators

> A real fairy tale, a tale in its true function, is a tale
> within a circle of listeners.
>
> Karel Čapek

A fairy tale keeps on the move between written and spoken
versions and back again, between print and performance
and, since the coming of mass media, between page and
screen; this peripatetic character confirms the sense that
the fairytale genre does not possess a precisely delineated
literary form, as does a novel by Jane Austen, but is as fluid as
a conversation taking place over centuries. The audience is
not necessarily assembled in one place at one moment—the
circle loops out across the centuries, forming a community
across barriers of language and nation as well as time. Think
of it as a plant genus, like roses or fungi or grasses, which
seed and root and flower here and there, changing species

and colour and size and shape where they spring. Or think of it as a tune, which can migrate from a voice to a symphony to a penny whistle, for a fairy tale does not exist in a fixed form or medium. The stories' interest isn't exhausted by repetition, reformulation, or retelling, but their pleasure gains from the endless permutations performed on the nucleus of the tale, its DNA as it were. C. S. Lewis, the creator of the Narnia books, pointed out that fairy tales don't even need to be especially well written to be unforgettable. Many of the most powerful tales are terse to the point of blankness, brimful of inconsistencies, and plotted with baffling lack of logic (why would a father decide to murder his twelve sons in favour of his daughter? why would another father cut off his daughter's hands?). Coleridge praised 'motiveless malignancy' in narrative; it certainly excites a frisson, that mixture of cold fear and thrilling transgressive pleasure that is the characteristic smoky aroma given off by fairy tales.

Mode Parisienne: Mother Goose Tales and Arabian Nights

In 1697, when Charles Perrault published *Contes du temps passé* (Tales of Olden Times), his classic anthology of seven fairy tales, he did not use his own name, but attributed the book to his son, describing how Pierre had written down stories he had heard told by nurses and old women. The subtitle, *Tales of Mother Goose*, picks up a proverbial phrase for an 'old wives' tale', an equivocal and ancient expression (Plato uses it) for traditional folk wisdom passed on by grannies and nurses. '*Contes de ma mère l'oye*' appears in the frontispiece of Perrault's first edition, written on a plaque hanging on the wall behind a crone sitting by the fire with children around her; it signals to the reader her character as a generic figure of the storyteller, a bardic repository of tribal lore.

Perrault's tales were soon translated into English and disseminated in unpretentious chapbooks, illustrated with tiny woodcuts of significant moments in the tales: the wolf springing on Red Riding Hood to devour her, Bluebeard dragging his wife by her hair with his scimitar raised menacingly (see Figure 8). The collection closed with 'Peau-d'âne' (Donkeyskin), in a prose version (Perrault had earlier refashioned it in light, ironic verse, insouciant and comic). It ends, in Angela Carter's translation, 'The story...is not something you might read every day in the morning papers. But as long as there are children, mothers, grandmothers and Mother Goose, it will always seem new.'

Such a fairy tale, with its dark theme of incest, was in this way firmly identified as family entertainment, with an emphasis on continuity through women's voices.

Perrault has become by far the most celebrated pioneer of the fashion for the literary fairy tale under the *ancien régime*, but he was only one writer among many. Fairy tales were taken up most enthusiastically by defenders of the '*modernes*' (French, local, demotic) against the '*anciens*' (classical, universal, latinate)—chiefly independent-minded women of courtly, élite society, *conteuses*, *salonnières*, and bluestockings who embroidered and expanded the generic plotlines and characters, adding rococo ornament to biting satire about domestic cruelty and political tyranny. Marie-Catherine D'Aulnoy, an extravagant and prolific writer, was immediately pirated in English translation; she was the first author to use the phrase *Contes des fées* (Tales of the Fairies), in 1698. In England, she was dubbed Mother Bunch, a name with a ring of Mother Goose, which summons false expectations of jolly fun; D'Aulnoy's writing is arch, worldly, and acerbic. The women fairytale writers were often loquacious, whereas Perrault is laconic; they were embattled, while he gives more of a Gallic shrug at the misdeeds of fairytale characters. Marie-Jeanne L'Héritier, Henriette-Julie de Murat, Charlotte-Rose de La Force, and Marguerite de Lubert likewise adopted the conventions of the fairy tale to depict the virtues, the sufferings—and the hopes—of their sex; they speak out against arranged marriages and the double standard, which allowed men to enjoy love affairs and punished women for adultery, which gave men an education and denied women the freedom that follows from knowledge; their heightened and sardonic flights of fancy about wealth and luxury also point to the excesses of the royal and princely courts. 'The White Cat' by D'Aulnoy contains a brilliantly savage account of one of Louis XIV's ruinous wars. Several of these women suffered legal penalties—prison, house arrest, exile—for their views, even though they had hidden their messages in apparent frippery.

In the same period, the *Arabian Nights* (Figure 6) began appearing in print for the first time. The Orientalist Antoine Galland subdued the effervescent original into courtly French with his masterly and hugely influential rendering (*Les Mille et une nuit*, 1704–17); its English counterpart, the so-called 'Grub Street' anonymous version (*Arabian Nights' Entertainments*), appeared soon after. Serialized in broadsheets and

47

Figure 6 Telling stories to save your life: Shahrazad's ultimately successful nocturnal stratagem. From a manuscript of *Alf layla wa-layla* (The Tales of the Thousand and One Nights), Baghdad, 16th century.

journals, it became a triumphant success, even a craze. Writers enthusiastically adopted the mode of Oriental fairy tale for the page and the stage. For example, fairytale motifs, travel fantasy, satires of political ambition and despotic excess, dreams of vast fortunes, and *commedia dell'arte* buffoonery are all mixed together in Alain-Reneé Lesage's *Arlequin roi des ogres ou Les Bottes de sept lieues* (Harlequin, King of the Ogres or the Seven-League Boots, 1720), in which a chorus of ogres chants nonsense 'in their native Algonquin'.

The confluence of the European fairy tale with the Orientalizing tale was crucial; many of the defining features of the genre crystallized in the process. In this way, popular fairy tale, with its roots in what was to be called folklore, intertwined and cross-fertilized with Oriental tales that had been refined by Galland's renderings. D'Aulnoy invokes 'an old Arab slavewoman' as her informant, for example, which may or may not have been the case. In the chapbooks Barbe bleue/Bluebeard is identified by illustrators as a Saracen (turbaned and brandishing a scimitar), and his last bride is given the name Fatima. The debt to the *Nights* has been underestimated. The Oriental mode of storytelling has inspired the excess and opulence, revenges and passions, animal metamorphoses and imbricated structure in, for example, Anthony Hamilton's burlesque 'The Ram', and D'Aulnoy's fairy tale 'The Blue Bird'. But these are two examples from a host that could be cited.

The late seventeenth and early eighteenth century marks the start of the modern fairy tale as we know it, and Perrault and Galland are the key exponents who, in the history of readership and reception, established as literature 'the Fairy

49

way of writing'. Collectors and writers like Perrault and, later, the Grimm Brothers, formed a corpus, even a canon, of fairy tales, and their printed versions established standard elements. When new storytellers later tackled 'Hansel and Gretel', they were consequently aware of a template in ways that a medieval storyteller might not have been.

Baroque Licence: Basile in Naples

The fashion for fairy writing was new and wildly popular, but the way of writing was old, as it turned out, and the *salonnières* and the Oriental taletellers who began filling volumes with their fairy tales belonged in a literary lineage. As Borges shows so incisively in his essay 'Kafka and his Precursors', the success of their way of telling reveals with hindsight the tradition's landmarks, and pioneers of the genre who have been—and in some cases remain—rather overlooked. Many of the enchantments, characters, and plotlines in the stories of Perrault, D'Aulnoy, et al. are first encountered in print in two ebullient Italian collections, *Le piacevoli notti* (The Pleasant Nights, 1550–5) by the Venetian Straparola, about whom very little is known, and in *Il Penta-merone ovvero lo cunto de li cunti* (The Pentameron, or Tale of Tales, 1634–6) by a Neapolitan, Giambattista Basile, a courtier and soldier. It's no accident that these two authors created their story cycles in great seaports, where cultures, languages, ideas—and above all travellers—met one another.

Both writers dramatize with witty irreverence the most outlandish scenes of magic and metamorphosis, and inter-twine them with real-life dramas of family rivalry and erotic passion, often in fantastic, exotic, and luxurious settings; their adult material flows through baroque, sophisticated, yet demotic prose, packed with fanciful imagery and proverbial turns of phrase; mandarin ironies, high-flown emotions fuse with crude jokes and japes to create a hybrid text, where preposterous entertainment meets lacerating cynicism about humankind. Basile distils a heady brew from Neapolitan dialect and courtly prose, all stuffed with proverbs, catches, and saws (not unlike Shakespeare, in this respect, and they are contemporaries in a humanist Europe, after all).

Not all fairy stories' endings are happy: in Straparola's forerunner of 'Puss-in-Boots', the hero forgets all about the (female) cat's help once he has become a prince. Early versions of 'Donkeyskin', Beast Bridegroom stories, 'Cinderella', 'Sleeping Beauty', and 'Rapunzel' also appear in these collections—again, with significant differences. Basile's Cinderella, for example, conspires to murder her stepmother so her dear governess can marry her father instead. But her plan fails when the governess produces seven children of her own, whom she favours over Cinderella.

Basile's title—*Il Pentamerone*—nods to Boccaccio's *Decameron* (Ten Days), and Basile also stages a storytelling scene: over the course of five days, ten crone storytellers, each savagely evoked in decrepitude and monstrosity, come forward one by one to tell fifty tales. The framing device, which holds the sprawling contents inside an overarching plot, is fundamental to the structure of the *Arabian Nights*, and has been much copied. In the view of the literary scholar Ros Ballaster, it defines the genre of the Oriental fairy tale. More importantly, it sets before us, the readers, a supposed

---

BOX 3 *'The Cinderella Cat', by Giambattista Basile*

'...the king, taking it [the slipper] in his hand, said, "If the basement indeed is so beautiful, what must the building be? O beauteous candlestick, where is the candle that consumes me? O tripod of the bright boiler in which life simmers! O beautiful cork, fastened to the angling-line of Love, with which he has caught my soul! Lo, I embrace you, I press you to my heart; and if I cannot reach the plant, I adore at least the roots; if I cannot possess the capital of the column, I kiss the base. You who until now were the prison of a white foot, are now the fetter of an unhappy heart."

'So saying he called his secretary, and commanded the trumpeter to sound a "Too, too!" and make proclamation, that all the women of that country should come to a feast and banquet which he had taken it into his head to give.'

Basile's storytelling manner mimics, with hyperbolic gusto, oral techniques of enumeration, rhythm, and decoration, eddying and whirling word clusters; he relishes bodily functions with a Rabelaisian appetite and likes the off-colour anecdote—these are stories in which a fart may be celebrated in raiment more usually reserved, in later literature, for the apparel of fairies. Both Straparola and Basile communicate a fabulous vision, filled with contrasting colours, buoyant with that *'leggerezza'* or lightness that Italo Calvino extols, combining horror, jests, and outrage, sweetness and irony, violence and cruelty. As Calvino wrote about Basile in his essay 'The Map of Metaphors' (1974): 'In the *Pentamerone*, there are pages of devastating sensual excitement...'

anterior oral storytelling scene. This is the essential point: fairy tales on the page invoke live voices, telling stories aloud. A memory of a living narrator reverberates in the genre, even when the story is manifestly a highly wrought literary text. Authors like Straparola and Basile and D'Aulnoy are playacting, stepping into the roles of Shahrazad or Mother Goose, because one of the things that fairy tale promises is an unbroken link with the past.

Several of Basile's stories reappear, with variations, in the Grimms' celebrated collection, *Children's and Household Tales*. Basile's opening, for example, features a magic donkey, table, and cudgel given to the simpleton hero by a doting ogre. The Italianist Nancy Canepa has suggested that this tale mirrors Basile's own strategy as a writer: he annexed tools of peasants' storytelling to perform enchanted acts of his own.

The distinction between genuine folk tales and literary fairy tales is difficult to maintain, faced with the metamorphoses of a single story—for example 'The Sleeping Beauty' or 'Ali Baba'. Scholars who refute popular, unlettered participants in the tales' history are staking too much on the literary record; the latter is interwoven in the dissemination of the story, in manuscript and print, and helps crystallize its features, but the case for the invention of an entire story, *ab ovo*, by an individual writer, flies in the face of the evidence—Plato mentions old women going down to the harbour to comfort the victims bound for the Minotaur's table by telling them stories, and in the second century AD Apuleius places his marvellous 'Tale of Cupid and Psyche' on the lips of an old and disreputable bawd. This is partly a point about social history:

people told stories before mass literacy; but it is also about desire: what is loved in stories is often an imagined link to a long, living lineage.

German Dreams: The Grimm Brothers

The Grimm Brothers' anthology staged a crucial encounter between the *Volk* (the People) and the intellectual élite; their processes of collecting and editing reveal very clearly the entanglement of sources in the modern making of the classic fairy tales. During the turbulent times of the Napoleonic invasions, the writer Clemens Brentano, his sister Bettina, and her husband, their collaborator Achim von Arnim, hungered for an authentic, homegrown, original literature, stemming from the *Volk*. Like Romantics elsewhere, they were caught in a hum of voices present and past; they were not lone innovators but members of a large movement of national and cultural rediscovery of 'that beautiful interest in wild tales, which made the child a man', in the words of the essayist Charles Lamb. Their shared interest lay with materials hitherto disregarded as low and vulgar: popular wisdom and fancy, from ballads to facetious jokes, homespun animal fables to fierce stories of revenge and justice. Von Arnim and Brentano's three-volume anthology of songs and ballads, *Des Knaben Wunderhorn* (The Boy's Wonderful Horn), filled with terrifying stories and desperate passions, first began appearing in 1805; as in Wordsworth and Coleridge's *Lyrical Ballads*, an eerie light of faerie glowed in the poems, and the frisson of cruel fate delivered brilliant dramatic effects. Schubert set 'The Erl-King', as transcribed by

Goethe, and the sound of the piano rushes like the hoary demon god of the wind, a death spectre, an ogre who snatches the boy riding pillion on his father's horse:

> 'I love you, your beautiful form entices me;
> And if you're not willing, then I will use force.'
> 'My father, my father, he's grabbing me now!
> The Erlking has done me harm!'

When Brentano and his circle heard about the Grimm Brothers' similar interests, they invited them to start collecting tales and to send them materials. The results have come to define fairy tale all over the world.

In 1812, the first edition of their anthology, comprising eighty-six stories, came out in an edition of 600, with an apparatus of notes running to hundreds of pages. It was not really intended to be read for pleasure at all by the children and households of its title; it was a learned work setting out to reconfigure the cultural history of Germany along lines that would emancipate it from the monopoly of classical and French superiority. Yet this collection—by the final, standard edition of 1857 the number of tales had grown to 210—was to become the most widely translated work in the world after the Bible and the Qur'an, rendered into more than 160 languages so far, including Xhosa and Tagalog, and still counting.

Here are the tall and trackless forests and the entranced castles, treacherous queens, murderous mothers, careless fathers, the magical bird that sings woe to evil-doers, the severed horse head that speaks the truth, gnomes and nixies, a queer little fellow like Rumpelstiltskin and a frog that wants to sleep on the princess's pillow, the empty bowls that miraculously fill, the well with heaven lying in its depths, the brave siblings, the self-laying festive tablecloth, the clever and friendly creatures and the ravenous beasts, the ruthless plots, the bleak, deadpan tone, the fatalism—and the joyful sudden turn of events, when the world is set to rights after horror. Here are the classics that have travelled the world: 'The Boy Who Wanted to Learn How to Shudder', 'Snow White', 'Foundling Bird', 'Hansel and Gretel', 'Little Redcap', 'The Girl with No Hands', 'The Singing Springing Lark', 'Ashypet', 'Fitcher's Bird', and 'The Juniper Tree'.

Germany wasn't yet Germany. It was a congeries made up of dozens of principalities and archdukedoms, free Hanseatic ports and archbishoprics. History shows us that the modern nation-state develops long after a national culture and its language: think of Italy and of Dante, writing five hundred years before Italian unification. For centuries, most of the peninsula had been under German or Austrian or Spanish rule, while the Renaissance, indisputably Italian, was influencing the whole world. The Grimms were living in a time of turmoil and bloodshed. The Revolution in France inspired corresponding fervour among some of their Romantic compatriots; then Napoleon, leading his abused and adoring armies to invade one European territory after another, took possession of the city of Kassel, where the brothers were working in the library, and installed as ruler his brother, Jerôme, as King of Westphalia.

One response to humiliation is to assert cultural riches and distinctiveness, even pre-eminence. The Grimms became part of the swelling movement to retrieve a record of the German spirit, through an encyclopaedic account of the German language, myths, history, customs, beliefs, and knowledge. They called it 'Folk Poesy', and they thought of it as part of nature—untutored, uncontaminated by book learning, wild as the forests and the mountains. In a 'Circular Letter', which Jacob Grimm sent out in 1815, he began by asking correspondents to find songs and rhymes, but he moved on swiftly to request the stories for which the Grimms have become the most widely read writers of fairy tales in the world. He specified 'Local Legends (*Sagen*) not in verse, most especially both the various Nurses' Tales and Children's Tales (*Ammen- und Kindermärchen*) of giants, dwarves, monsters, king's sons and daughters spellbound and set free, devils, treasures and wishing objects...Animal Fables in particular are to be noted...'.

The Grimms stipulated that 'Folk Poesy' must be unadulterated in its origins: 'Above all,' wrote Jacob, 'it is important that these items should be gathered faithfully and truly, without decoration and addition and with the greatest possible precision and detail, from the mouths of the storytellers, where practicable in and with their own authentic words...' (Figure 7).

They themselves went around the country gathering tales, resembling the fairy tales' own protagonists who set out to pick mushrooms and find kindling in the depths of the forests. In Marburg, for example, the university town where they were students, they visited the hospital where an old woman was celebrated for her repertoire, but they found she didn't want to pass on her lore to the fine young

Figure 7 *Sources and gossip: women, children (and others) pass on the wisdom of the tribe. Paula Rego,* Secrets and Stories, *1989.*

scholars. So the brothers persuaded the little daughter of the hospital director to ask her for a story and bring it back to them—the result was 'Aschenputtel', the German 'Cinderella', in which the sisters cut off their heels and cut off their toes, before their eyes are put out one by one by the doves which have acted to help Cinderella throughout, the agents of her dead mother.

This is the cruellest variant of the famous story, and perhaps the old woman did not want the élite young men to see into the secret thoughts and dreams of revenge that generations of women have entertained?

The brothers were questing for a true original and were filled with confidence that they would find a local, pristine, authentic tradition. They kept worrying at their material, so that in effect they rewrote what they collected into the form of the fairy tale—terse, affectless, peculiar, violent, and bafflingly illogical.

But very soon doubts began about the unadulterated German character of the material: so many of their sources were literate, even French-speaking, sophisticates and much-travelled, and the Grimms were rattled by the correspondences and echoes. So they pulled one story and then another from the first edition: more than thirty tales were set aside for failing the nationality test, including 'Puss-in-Boots' and 'The Sleeping Beauty'. Stories were migrants, blow-ins, border-crossers, tunnellers from France and Italy and more distant territories where earlier and similar stories had been passed on in Arabic and Persian and Chinese and Sanskrit.

The quest for authenticity was a vertiginous experience, and the concept of a home culture was engulfed, replaced by a hubbub of voices, the narrative melée of the past jostling to find a place to speak for the present. Reading the Grimms can feel like a dreamscape where faces from different times are all jumbled, assembling and disassembling, crystallizing and melting, moving in so close as to lose focus and then evaporating—plots and motifs, monsters and princesses, elves and spirits from the *Arabian Nights*, from the Neapolitan Basile, from Boccaccio all jostling as in Bottom's dream. In 'Strong Hans', this scene comes straight from an encounter with jinn: 'each of the air spirits seized one of the hairs on his head, and then began to fly upwards'.

The problem of authenticity was even more acute because several of the Grimms' sources were educated and well-travelled women (and some men), themselves informed by contacts, crosscurrents, and migrations. The brothers gathered several from a cousin, known as 'die alte Marie' (Old Mary), code for the authentic voice of the *Volk*. A tailor's widow, Dorothea Viehmann, became the most famous of their storytellers, her image on the frontispiece of their book.

She told them the very strange story 'Hans My Hedgehog', and its performative potential shows in the repetitions of motifs and reprises, in the frightening and playful episodes, as the storyteller makes-believe that she—or he—is pricking the child with the animal's quills.

Not content with purifying the German tradition, Wilhelm began altering other stories because they were off-colour by the standards of the day (Rapunzel bedded and pregnant before she's wedded!). The most acute quandary, however, that Wilhelm faced was how to make the transition to the page and keep the sense of the pristine origin. The brothers claimed that they were reproducing the voice of immemorial tradition, but Wilhelm shaped and polished, cadenced and ornamented many of the best-known tales over the course of nearly fifty years; above all, he censored the stories' frankness about sex, but let the violent reprisals stand. Eventually the brothers created the memorable tales in the form that has travelled the world.

Comparison of the 1812 versions with the fuller, patterned 1857 final, now standard, edition shows that Wilhelm had a fine sense of narrative dynamics, and the tales benefited hugely from his multiple interferences. 'The Frog

King', the opening tale of the book, first filled a single sparse paragraph. It now begins, 'In the olden days, when wishing still worked, there lived a king whose daughters were all beautiful, but the youngest daughter was so lovely that even the sun . . . was struck with wonder . . .'. These phrases strike what sounds like the pure note of fairy tale, but they are Wilhelm's invention, and they breathe necessary air and fancy into the bare opening of the original, 'There was once a king's daughter . . .' (1812). This phrase was itself an improvement on the earliest transcript of all (1810), which sounds as flat as a Jack and Jill reading book: 'The king's daughter went out into the forest . . .'.

Similarly, Antoine Galland had made scanty notes in his journal after hearing his source, Hanna Diab, tell 'Aladdin' or 'Ali Baba', and then later, through a similar literary process of expansive dramatization, enrichment, and elaboration, produced the lengthy early written versions, which themselves have been pulled and pushed into different shapes ever since.

Travelling Tales or Collective Unconscious?

Arguments still carry on between the diffusionists, who believe stories travel, and the universalists, who propose a collective unconscious. Formalists like the Russian Vladimir Propp and, later, structuralists like Claude Lévi-Strauss, influentially argued there were only this number of stories, or that number of plots. It is accepted wisdom that there are only seven stories and all the rest are variations on them (the first archive in Britain dedicated to Children's Literature, founded in Newcastle in 2005, is called Seven Stories). This view can only be maintained, I feel, by taking a very blunt approach, and differences between versions and the context which shapes them now command critical interest far more than basic similarities: several recent studies of 'Bluebeard' explore very fruitfully the tale's transformations. A picture book of the fairy tale for the early reading market, the Bartók opera *Bluebeard's Castle* with a libretto by the fabulist Béla Balázs, and the witty and perverse low-budget film, *Barbebleue* (2009), directed by Geneviève Breillat, hold far more fascination for their divergences than their structural identity. Conditions of conflict and flux in the contemporary world, alongside economic migration and global business mobility have also brought squarely to the foreground the restless movement of cultural expressions. Theories about world literature, of which fairy tale is a fundamental part, emphasize the porousness of borders, geographical and linguistic: no frontier can keep a good story from roaming. It will travel, and travel far, and travel back again in a different guise, a changed mood, and, above all, a new meaning.

In one sense, however, the Grimm Brothers created what they set out to discover. Their fairytale findings shaped a cultural identity for their country that readers and audiences, interpreters on stage, screen, for the eye and for the ear, recognize and associate with Germany, and not entirely to the advantage of the nation and its place in the cultural imaginary. The callous violence, cruelty, bizarre and extreme solutions produce a shiver no matter how many times you hear or read the stories. Even when they unfold a plot found in several other languages, the Grimm versions have a particular flavour and an unmistakable tone that compels attention and excites mixed feelings—a kind of guilty excitement at the heartless, even blithe outcomes. It's a tone of voice many subsequent writers have imitated—it reverberates in Margaret Atwood and her revisionings of myth and fairy tale. Philip Pullman invokes the American poet James Merrill yearning for 'the kind of unseasoned telling found | In legends, fairy tales, a tone licked clean | Over the centuries by mild old tongues, | Grandam to cub, serene, anonymous'. He wanted to capture this in prose, Pullman declares in the introduction to his 2012 translation of the Grimms. Yet the brothers were themselves kindly, restrained, peaceable souls. When death did come, first for Wilhelm in 1859, Jacob was disconsolate; he followed his brother four years later, in 1863. He was still hard at work on their vast Dictionary, and had only reached the letter F and the word for Fruit, *Frucht*. In many ways, they were looking to fairy tales for a binding common legacy, and for solace, light, and harmony; what they found there was a different kind of fruit, and yet the peculiar horror of their tales has brought an intense form of joy to multitudes of readers and listeners.

The dream of a pure fountainhead, of the old crone story-teller passing on the wisdom of the tribe, is an axiom of cultural nationalism, as well as a form of Romantic Pastoral that still runs through present-day writings of place and memory. But fairy tales, as the Grimms discovered, have no more sense of nation or native tongue than swifts or butterflies, and have proved stubborn and repeating emigrants, always slipping across borders (and back again).

Even when mass literacy was still on the distant horizon, popular storytelling existed in symbiosis with written variations, and the transition to the page gave every copyist itchy fingers. Rhythm, metre, refrain, and rhyme helped texts to set in a certain form, but as the myriad variations of a single ballad show, tellers and singers keep ringing their own changes. Pullman echoes this forcefully when he insists that the connection to voice must not be lost: 'A fairy tale is not a text.'

In *The Invention of Literature* (1999), the classical scholar Florence Dupont reminds us that many of the greatest works of human imagination were created to be performed, to be heard. Before the printing press and mass literacy, the written versions existed as blueprints or records of performances, recitals, speeches, songs, and other forms of oral communication. Voicing was an art of living creators, and the voice of the storyteller was polyphonous; the stories created were all different and the same at one and the same time—again the fairy tale as tune, riffed by singers or instrumentalists. Every listener is potentially a new storyteller. Early literature was not composed of fixed texts, but of play scripts and prompt books, storytellers' scrolls, pattern books. This certainly applies to the *Arabian Nights* and to the corpus of well-known fairy tales: storytellers remember the stories from having experienced them—heard or read—and they then recast them. However, the records were fluid and the work constantly re-created as it was passed on. In the same way as we hear a version of the Fall of Troy from the bard Demodocus in the *Odyssey* and another told by Aeneas to Dido in Virgil's *Aeneid*, so 'La Belle au bois dormant',

Perrault's surprisingly gory 'Sleeping Beauty', is only one permutation on a persistent theme.

Literature was a speech act performed by living voices present to their audiences, as in many public events today, when literary festivals put growing pressure on writers to become public performers. Writing, according to Dupont's argument, represented an attempt to capture the living voices in the work. Every story is an act of memory that communicates the living presence of its subjects. This turns books into death masks, she suggests, entombing the once living beings that made the sounds of the words. In the absence of those bodies, writing is fated to draw attention endlessly to that absence. The imagined presence of Old Mother Goose or '*die alte Marie*' or another narrator stages a strong attempt to keep continuity with a past when the tale was spoken and its teller was alive. Almost every collection of fairy tales pretends that they were told by someone who had it from someone who had it at first hand, once upon a time.

At a crucial moment in literary history, the earnest and scholarly Grimm Brothers acted as keepers of the records, like the scribes whom Caliph Haroun al-Rashid commands in the *Arabian Nights* to write down Shahrazad's stories in letters of gold, and place them in the palace library. Nineteenth-century collectors set out to capture the national imagination of their country, but time has revealed them to have been unwitting internationalists. The example of the Grimms set off a train of imitations: at a varying pace, all over the world, writers collected national or tribal fairy tales. In keeping with the political idealism of the earliest period of Romanticism, this literature of the illiterate became the foundation stone of a theory of cultural distinct-iveness. The stories offered rich deposits of memory, uncon-taminated, it was hoped, by learned imports. Giuseppe Pitrè, a doctor in Messina, Sicily, equipped his carriage with a spe-cial desk, writing equipment, and seating arrangements so he could gather stories from his patients as he made his rounds: Agatuzza Messia, who was his former nanny and worked as a quilt maker and laundress, was his chief source: 'She is far from beautiful, but is glib and eloquent; she has an appealing way of speaking, which makes one aware of her extraordinary memory and talent. Messia is in her seventies, is a mother, grand-mother, and great-grandmother; as a little girl she heard stories from her grand-mother, whose own mother had told them . . . [she] can't read, but she knows lots of things others don't.'

In the same town, Laura Gonzenbach, daughter of a pros-perous textile merchant who later served as the Swiss consul, also took down stories from her friends and neighbours, and translated their Sicilian into High German for publication in 1870. Through Gonzenbach's retellings, Sicilian Orientalism flows north again, and meets the streams of story spreading across Europe as a result of the German Romantics' success. Jack Zipes quotes a letter in which she writes, 'I've not been able to capture the genuine charm of these tales that lies in the manner and way the tales are told by these Sicilian women. Most of them . . . act out the entire plot with their hands . . . they even stand up and walk around the room when it's appropriate. They never use "he says" because they change the people's voices always through intonation.'

Calvino makes a similar point in the introduction to the magnificent collection, *Fiabe Italiane*; but his instincts as an original writer led him to abandon the dream of fidelity to the source. Instead, he rewrote all the stories from start to finish, trying to keep a feel for the voices he had encountered in the dusty back rooms of Italian provincial archives, voices whose vitality and brilliance he acknowledges fully in his Introduction. All the same, when Calvino decided to combine and re-imagine the material in the interests of literature, he stepped into the writerly tradition of Basile and Perrault, and his volume's lasting richness and fluency confirms his judgement.

In Russia, many collectors followed the Grimms' lead, mapping a national heritage through stories. Alexander Afanasyev, the most widely read today, published his stupendous anthology of around 600 fairy tales between 1855 and 1867. Chronology does not indicate which tales come first; many Russian fairy tales are unique, but again polyphony breaks out, as the stories echo with others from the circumpolar regions and the cultures along the Silk Road, intertwining with fairy tales from India, Central Asia, the Middle East, and from among the Lapps and Tungus.

In the English-speaking world, the Grimms' emulators were slower on the uptake, but once under way, folklore—the cartography and anthropology of the imagination—became a Victorian enthusiasm, alongside the imperial and scientific mapping adventures of the age. Joseph Jacobs assembled two influential volumes, *English Fairy Tales* (1890) and *More English Fairy Tales* (1894); he retells the Scottish 'Cinderella', in which the heroine is not covered in ashes, but wears a coat of rushes. Her mother feeds her and cares for her in the shape of a cow whose ears miraculously produce sustenance; this Cinders goes to the kirk, not the ball, where she catches the eye of the local laird. In this period, too, Charlotte Guest pieced and patched the Welsh *Mabinogion*, interweaving some of the strangest and fiercest wonder tales yet told.

The Blue Fairy Book and Ever After

The Romantic ideal of national heritage was however overstepped when Andrew Lang embarked on the coloured *Fairy Books* (1889–1912). He jumbled everything together, wherever the tale came from, then passed it all through an editing process under the direction of his wife, Leonora Alleyne, and a team of mostly women writers and translators, who standardized the prose for parental imprimatur. There are flashes of inspiration in the general Edwardian mannerliness: in Miss Minnie Wright's succinct version of D'Aulnoy's 'Princess Rosette', she replaces the long tongue-in-cheek *moralité* (originally targeting the Sun King) with the happiness of the princess's dog Frisk (for French *Frétillon*, wagging [its tail]), who 'never had anything worse than the wing of a partridge for dinner all the rest of his life'.

After *The Blue Fairy Book* came out in 1889, Andrew Lang was taken by surprise at the book's huge success and, in response to overwhelming readers' enthusiasm, agreed to bring out another, *The Red Fairy Book*, the very same year. But demand was still not satisfied, and he built a series of twelve volumes all told.

Lang wrote copiously and thought deeply about fairy tales, but even though he supported the distinction between oral, anonymous folk tales and literary production, he tumbled together, pell-mell, romances, myths, legends, episodes from the sagas, *fabliaux*, and fables from dozens of different sources of various kinds. He sifted ethnographical records to find stories that had once been told aloud, like the *Arabian Nights*, as well as translating stories that were literary in origin like the fairy tales of French *conteuses*. His accumulations re-kindled acquaintance with the population of giants, selkies, and brownies indigenous to Britain, with the kraken, ogres, and trolls from Scandinavia, Koschey the Deathless and Baba Yaga from the Russian forests, and a whole population of goblins and dragons. Lang had an inclusive, generous, world-embracing picture of the nations, flattened onto a plane of an eternal, monolithic past where making up fairy tales signified the human, and the stories joined us up together across time, modern society with ancient, contemporary with primordial. He declared:

> The natural people, the folk, has supplied us, in its unconscious way, with the stuff of all our poetry, law, ritual: and genius has selected from the mass, has turned customs into codes, nursery tales into romance, myth into science... ballad into epic...The student of this lore can look back and see the long-trodden way behind him, the winding tracks through the marsh and the forest and over burning sands. He sees the caves, the camps, the village, the towns where the race has tarried, for shorter time or longer, strange places many of them, and strangely haunted, desolate dwellings and inhospitable...

Yet, as Francis Spufford points out in his perceptive and unusual memoir, *The Child that Books Built* (2003), by the time of *Domesday Book* in 1086, it would have already been impossible for Hansel and Gretel to walk more than four miles through any English wood without bursting back out into open fields. The landscape of fairy tales is symbolic: 'The forest is where you are when your surroundings are not mastered.'

The coloured *Fairy Books* sequence has been of inestimable influence: with their haunting Pre-Raphaelite wood engravings by H. J. Ford, they aren't simply anthologies of powerful stories: they redefined for Victorians and their successors the scope and flavour of fairy tale itself as a genre. They were also hugely influential in their premise that a universal human imagination generated narratives that resembled one another far more closely than they differed, and in their wake, fairy books of stories from all over the world began to appear— Chinese, Japanese, Gipsy, Maori, and from different peoples in Africa, Australasia, India, the Caribbean, and every sub-division within national borders. Echoes are continually struck between a Palestinian tale, say, and an Inuit, though social contexts always shape the material, and the correspondences arise from the traffic of cultures, carried by many forces, including missionaries, ethnographers, and empire-builders.

The *Fairy Books* have also provided rich ore for generations of writers, composers, and artists. Angela Carter acknowledged their impact on her when she was young; Jeanette Winterson in her novels *The Passion* (1987) and *Sexing the Cherry* (1989), introduces numerous fairytale motifs, including the shoes that are mysteriously worn out every morning (from 'The Twelve Dancing Princesses' found in *The Red Fairy Book*); recently the composer Jonathan Dove with the writer Alan Middleton created a wonderfully upbeat panto from *The Enchanted Pig*, a tale found in Basile but included by Lang in a Romanian folk version he had tracked down.

'Experience which is passed on from mouth to mouth', writes Walter Benjamin, 'is the source from which all story-tellers have drawn.' He continues, 'And among those who have written down the tales, it is the great ones whose written version differs least from the speech of the many nameless storytellers.' This should be modified to read, 'whose written version *sounds as if* it differs least from the speech...'.

For every new literary adventurer in the forests of fairy tale, keeping the voice in the story direct and lively presents the chief difficulty. Angela Carter in *The Bloody Chamber* (1979) swerves into the first person—with brilliant, dramatic, buttonholing effect: 'My father lost me to the beast at cards' opens one of her variations on 'Beauty and the Beast', a fairy tale that turns up in the Grimms under the lovely riddling title, 'The Singing, Springing Lark'. Another Grimm tale ('The Goose Girl at the Spring') suddenly breaks off towards the end, '...the trouble is, my grandmother, who told it to me, is losing her memory, and she's forgotten the rest'. It's a polished moment of intimacy, maybe true, maybe not, but in any case none of the sources—the tale is first found in print in 1833 in an Austrian dialect version, then in 1840 in High German—thought of cutting this touch of authenticity and filling in the plot. Some of the other stories end with the storyteller breaking in; 'Hansel and Gretel' closes with the happy nonsense rhyme:

> The Mouse has run
> The tale is done—
> And if you can catch it, you can make yourself a great
> big furry hat.

The lines are a promise and a prophecy: the narrator is there ('Crick crack, break your back'), and the tale will never be caught, but will run and run. As has been the case, since 'Hansel and Gretel' has been revisited in every medium and the story has become proverbial.

The folklorists of the nineteenth century laid too much emphasis on a national *Geist* (spirit) expressed by stories told in a certain language, and their model of oppositions between textual and oral transmission, popular and polite origins, literate writers and illiterate tellers, was starkly schematic and has been superseded. The flow and contraflow between voice and page and back again have been incessant in the history of the literature of enchantment, while performance, from antique oratory to present-day video games, has always conducted such stories from a fixed script to fluid narration in different forms. When fairy tales have authors—Hans Christian Andersen, Alan Garner or Philip Pullman, Margaret Atwood or Angela Carter, however invented the tale may be, the writers frequently invoke their forerunners and characterize themselves as garrulous old gossips, popular, anonymous, authentic contacts to a past world where fairy tales were the living literature that everyone knew.

4

Potato Soup

True Stories/Real Life

The meaning [of the tales] has long ago been lost, but it is still felt, giving the tale its substance, while at the same time satisfying our pleasure in the marvellous. They are never merely the shimmering colours of insubstantial fantasy.

Jacob and Wilhelm Grimm

In the 1950s, Italo Calvino embarked on doing for Italian literature what the Grimms had done a century before in Germany. Italian bundles fairy tale, folk tale, and fable into the word *fiaba*, and Calvino was an impassioned advocate of the whole range of stories, and hunted for them in every source he could find. In the introduction to *Fiabe Italiane* (1956; translated as *Italian Folk Tales*), he wrote, 'Now that the book is finished, I know that this was not a hallucination . . . but the confirmation of something I already suspected—folktales (*fiabe*) are real.'

What did Calvino mean by this assertion? He is the most inspired and fantastical of modern fabulists, author of masterly and complex works of contemporary fiction such as *If on a Winter's Night a Traveller* and *Invisible Cities*, but he had begun his career writing novels and short stories of sensitive Chekhovian observation. His encounter with *la fiaba* was a revelation to him, and wrought a momentous change in his approach to fiction: as a member of the partisans who fought Fascism and a communist in Italy after the war, he saw fantastic fiction as the literature of the people whom he wanted to reach and represent. When he proclaims 'Folktales are real (*le fiabe sono vere*)' he means that they speak of poverty, scarcity, hunger, anxiety, lust, greed, envy, cruelty, and of all the grinding consequences in the domestic scene and the larger picture. The structures of wonder and magic open ways of recording experience while imagining a time when suffering will be over. Fate will be changed; perpetrators overcome. The wishful thinking and the happy ending are rooted in sheer misery. When he writes that he became obsessed with the fairy tale about a donkey that shits gold, he might have been invoking a symbol for the form itself, a humble, low thing that brings amazement and riches.

Pins, Lice, Mice, & Want

Princes and queens, palaces and castles dominate the foreground of a fairy tale, but through the gold and glitter, the depth of the scene is filled with vivid and familiar circumstances, as the fantastic faculties engage with the world of experience. Realism of content also embraces precise observation of detail, and contrasts between earthiness and preposterous fancy sharpen the entertaining effect. Perrault tells us, for example, that the cruel sisters have dressmakers' pins from England, the most fashionable and most coveted article at the time. In the Grimms' 'The Three Golden Hairs', the Devil himself is the adversary, and hell is a kitchen much like any ordinary kitchen where his granny sits by the stove. When the brave hero appears, a poor lad who's been set an impossible task by the proud princess to fetch her the trophy (the hairs in the title), Granny is kind to him, and turns the boy into an ant to keep him safe. She hides him in the folds of her apron until she has herself pulled out the three hairs, shushing the Devil as she does so. She then turns our hero back again into human form and sends him back to the world above to marry the princess.

It is emblematic that the Devil's kind old granny can pull out the required hairs because she is busy de-lousing him, something that's comforting even in Hell. Each of the three hairs then brings about a blessing that makes a joke of the story's roots in toil and hunger: with the first, the Devil reveals that a spring has dried up because an old toad is squatting on a stone that's blocking it; with the second that an apple tree no longer bears fruit because a mouse is nibbling through its roots; and with the third that the ferry-man who's working day in and day out, poling passengers across the river need only put his pole in the hands of one of his passengers to be free.

Many fairy tales about golden-haired princesses with tiny feet still address the difficulty, in an era of arranged marriage and often meagre resources, of choosing a beloved and being allowed to live with him or her. Many explore other threats all too familiar to the stories' receivers: the loss of a mother in childbirth is a familiar, melancholy opening to many favourites.

Behind their gorgeous surfaces you can glimpse an entire history of childhood and the family: the oppression of landowners and rulers, foundlings, drowned or abandoned children, the ragamuffin orphan surviving by his wits, the maltreated child who wants a day off from unending toil, or the likely lad who has his eye on a girl who's from a better class than himself, the dependence of old people, the rivalries between competitors for love and other sustenance. Unlike myths, which are about gods and superheroes, fairytale protagonists are recognizably ordinary working people, toiling at ordinary occupations over a long period of history, before industrialization and mass literacy. In the *Arabian Nights* the protagonists belong to more urban settings, and practise trades and commerce. Some are abducted and then sold into slavery, many are cruelly driven by their masters— and mistresses. In the European material, the drudgery is more rural, the enslavement unofficial and more personal in its cruelty. It is fair to say that fairytale heroines are frequently skivvies who take on the housework uncomplainingly, and that this kind of story won favour in the Victorian era and later, at the cost of eclipsing lively rebel protagonists, tricksters like Finette (Finessa in English translation), who turns the tables on her sisters' seducers, or Marjana the slave girl who pours boiling oil on the Forty Thieves.

Direct and shared experiences of material circumstances— of the measures that sociologists use to establish the well-being of a given society—are taken up by fairy tales as a matter of course: when the mother dies giving birth, that child will have to survive without her love and protection, and that is a grim sentence. The pot of porridge that is never empty speaks volumes about a world where hunger and want and dreadful toil are the lot of the majority, whose expectations are rather modest by contemporary standards. 'A fairy tale', Angela Carter once remarked, 'is a story in which one king goes to another king to borrow a cup of sugar.'

D. H. Lawrence famously proclaimed, 'Trust the tale, not the teller.' To which Jeanette Winterson retorts, repeating again and again, 'I'm telling you stories. Trust me.' But in what ways can we trust the tale—and even trust the teller? How can such preposterous fantastic stories be true, as Calvino and others who value fairy tales have claimed?

One answer is that a story is an archive, packed with history: just as an empty field in winter can reveal, to the eyes of an ancient archaeologist, what once grew there, how long ago the forest was cleared to make way for pasture, and where the rocks that were picked out of the land eventually fetched up, so a fairy tale bears the marks of the people who told it over the years, of their lives and their struggles.

C. S. Lewis writes that in literature there is realism of presentation on the one hand, and realism of content on the other: 'The two realisms are quite independent. You can get that of presentation without that of content, as in medieval romance: or that of content without that of presentation, as in French (and some Greek) tragedy; or both together, as in *War and Peace*; or neither, as in the *Furioso* or *Rasselas* or *Candide*.'

According to these distinctions, it is possible to see how fairy tales, while being utterly fantastical in presentation, are forthright in their realism as to what happens and can happen.

Mothers died in childbirth, and large families of step-relations arose as a result, competing for resources. In fairy tales, want stalks everyone, and the word's double meaning matters: both desire and lack. Measures taken to meet want are often extreme, but injustices are endemic in a society that's itself unfair, with hierarchies decreed chiefly by blood and accidents of birth. People steal and brawl and cheat— and sometimes the story is on the side of the cheats. The word of fathers, husbands, and even of younger brothers is law.

Fairy tales from cultures in which polygamy was practised reflect it: rivalry between co-wives over their children's future caused vicious conflicts, a situation reproduced in the Chinese 'Cinderella' (recorded in the ninth century, and the earliest variant extant): Yeh-hsien suffers miseries at the hands of her father's co-wife, not under the regime of a new stepmother. Where dowries were crucial for a young woman to get married, dowries figure vividly in fairy tales: in Basile's sparkling 'Pinto Smalto' (Painted Bread), Betta tells her father that if he is so keen she should marry, he must give her a fabulous *corredo* (trousseau)—jewels, gold, silks, etc. But she also stipulates flour, sugar, and rosewater. She then bakes a cake in the shape of a gorgeous young man, who comes to life. The story continues through various misadventures but ends gloriously.

Family Secrets

When the eldest son, according to the law of primogeniture, inherited everything, the younger brother would set out on his adventures penniless, to return fabulously endowed, as in the Grimms' 'The Boy Who Wanted to Learn How to Shudder'. The genre's themes are real-life themes and the passions real-life passions: getting by and getting what you want, knowing the odds are stacked and that all might be lost . . . Luck is powerful, but resourcefulness, often amoral, is praiseworthy. The situations in fairy tales also capture deep terrors of occurrences common and, mercifully, uncommon.

Unspeakable—unbelievable—acts are also always taking place. Terrible family violence: a father cuts off his daughter's hands, because the Devil wants to carry her off; another daughter disguises herself in a coat of animal hides after her father wants to marry her. Small children are damaged: Hansel and Gretel are abandoned by their mother and father to die in the woods and then narrowly escape a cannibal witch. And so on. These are acts which contradict all ideas of natural feeling. But these situations, however horribly they beat belief, have been spoken of in the stories, and they are echoed, week by week, in the news. When a child dies at the hands of parents who have starved and tortured him, as in the case of Daniel Pelka, and nobody moves to help him; when young girls are kidnapped and held prisoner by an apparently ordinary man in an ordinary American suburb; and when Josef Fritzl imprisons his daughter in a cellar and keeps her there for twenty-four years, fathering seven children on her until he was discovered in 2008, then fairy tales can be recognized as witnesses to every aspect of human nature. They also act to alert us—or hope to.

Starvation and infanticide are recurrent dangers, and their victims devise ways of opposing them, avenging themselves on the perpetrators, and of turning the status quo upside down. The plots convey messages of resistance—a hope of escape.

The siren function of the form, saying the unsayable and tolling a warning in the night, has been lessened in recent years, when child abuse has come to be recognized, and appalling cases of cruelty, involving incest, enslavement, and rape, are made known by other means. Fairy tales used to be a rare witness to such crimes, and encode them cryptically for the younger generation to absorb, but they can now watch them unfold in the media. However, recognition and familiarity with the possibility does not seem to have sharpened sensitivity or produced change, only increased a general fear for children's safety. Fairy tales used to transmute the horrors by setting them once upon a time and far away, and in this way did not directly raise the spectre of a killer next door but smuggled in their warnings under cover of magical storytelling.

Social historians have drawn on the tales for evidence about conditions of life in the past. Eugen Weber wrote 'Fairies and Hard Facts: The Reality of Folktales' (1981), an article which proved very influential. Robert Darnton, in a chapter of his sparkling book *The Great Cat Massacre* (1984), also emphasizes the true witness of Mother Goose. Weber's title is echoed, for example, by Maria Tatar in her study *The*

Hard Facts of the Grimms' Fairy Tales (1987). Jack Zipes, the most industrious scholar in the field, has developed a politically committed, cultural materialist perspective which explores the multiple ricochets between historical facts and *mentalités* (including class and gender values) with fairytale scenarios. His extensive criticism, from *Don't Bet on the Prince* (1986) to the recent *The Irresistible Rise of the Fairy Tale* (2012) has simultaneously helped give fairy tales greater stature as literature and led to sharp controversy about their pernicious or liberating influence on audiences and readers, especially the young. This opens one of the most charged questions about fairy tales: not, do they carry the evidence and reflect what happens? But do they interact with reality and shape it? Are they addressing the future as well as the past?

The French novelist Michel Tournier (who is steeped in fairy tale), has distinguished between the French terms *conte*, *fable*, and *nouvelle* (this last meaning a short story as well as a news item) regarding their relation to reality. *Fables*, as in Aesop and La Fontaine's animal parables, are 'transparent' in their explicit moral lessons, while *nouvelles* report on the facts. Both destroy all interest in the stories they tell by what he calls their 'brutal opacity'—their obviousness. By contrast, *contes*, Tournier declares, have 'crystalline translucency', which allows glimpses of truths but does not state them—this is the seduction and power of fairy tale.

Tournier has frequently revisited monsters and ogres in his fiction, including Bluebeard, who offers a fruitful test case for his concept of fairy tale as a vehicle of translucent insights.

Figure 8 Serial killer, jealous husband, or regular patriarch? *La Barbe bleue*, from *Le Cabinet des fées*, ed. C. J. Mayer, illustrated by Clément-Pierre Marillier 1785–9.

Extreme Crimes: Bluebeard, Serial Killer

Bluebeard (Figure 8) has become a familiar character, whatever the medium, whatever the date: in opera, cartoon, X-rated film, or graphic novel, he is an archetypal serial murderer, terrifying and yet alluring. Men and women have responded equally, showing strong identification from different vantage points.

'When he was gone she walked about the house from top to bottom, inspecting everything. At last she came to the forbidden door. She looked at the key, she put it in the lock. But what did she see as she went in? A huge blood-stained basin was standing in the middle of the room, and in it there lay human beings, dead and chopped in pieces.'

But is Perrault's *La Barbe bleue* a tale of thrilling terror, born of fantasy, or could it have roots in fact? Could such extreme tales really have a basis in history, in the lived experience of men and women?

The Bluebeard figure who appears in Grimm is a less ambiguous villain. The emphasis falls squarely on the dangers of marriage, and the tales feature a plucky trickster heroine who gets the better of her would-be murderous groom. He figures in two of their most mysterious and powerful stories, 'Fitcher's Bird', and 'The Robber Bridegroom', one of the earliest stories the Grimms collected.

A rich man turns up and asks to marry a miller's beautiful daughter. She doesn't take to him, and when she's making her way to his house, deep in the heart of a dark forest, her forebodings grow very heavy. A friendly bird sounds the alarm:

> 'Turn back, turn back, my pretty young bride,
> In a house of murderers you've arrived.'

But she goes in all the same, and finds every room entirely empty, except for a doddery old woman in the cellar, who cries out, 'The only wedding you'll celebrate is a wedding with death.'

When her fiancé returns with his gang, they're dragging another young woman with them, and our heroine watches from her hiding place as they make their victim drink— 'three glasses full, one white, one red, one yellow, and before long her heart burst in two. The robbers tore off her fine clothes, put her on the table, chopped her beautiful body into pieces, and sprinkled them with salt.'

They also chop off one of her fingers wearing a gold ring, but it flies through the air and lands in our heroine's lap. She makes her escape, and in the perfect dénouement, she tells the guests at her own wedding feast how she has suffered from a terrible nightmare, and describes the horrors she witnessed. When she reaches the end, she presents her groom with the severed finger. He realizes he's been unmasked, and tries to run. The guests seize him and turn him over to the law; he and his robber band are executed for their dreadful deeds.

This grisly tale communicates, beneath the Gothic scenes, several different layers of historical truth. It reveals many aspects of marriage in Europe in the past, and expresses resistance to the usual customs, conveying the apprehension of the girl who leaves her home to live far away in her husband's house; it takes for granted the power and attraction of money, and it confronts her lack of choice in the matter. The picture of a cannibal gang goes much further than the serial murders in Perrault's *La Barbe bleue*, but by stacking the evidence against the bridegroom, this version makes a very strong case for giving power to decide to the bride.

In the other Grimm Bluebeard tale, called 'Fitcher's Bird', the murderer is a wizard, or, in some translations, a warlock; a very close variation, 'Silver Nose', is also included by Calvino, and both feature spirited heroines who are possessed of mother wit—and a ferocious instinct for survival. Their defiance of the tyrant should be read in school assemblies to help young people to resist older men—and sometimes women—who get them in their clutches.

Historians have looked for connections beyond ordinary conditions, to identify actual events and known individuals at the root of a certain fairy tale. Two of the best known of all—'Bluebeard' and 'Snow White'—have been linked to individuals whose lives reveal deep causes for tensions in private and public arenas.

Most prominently, Bluebeard has been identified with Gilles de Rais, the Breton commander who fought alongside Joan of Arc in the Hundred Years' War and was condemned to be hanged for sorcery and satanic abuse—the ritual murder of scores, perhaps hundreds, of children at his castle (he was spared burning because he was a nobleman). George Bernard Shaw even included him under that name in his play, *Joan of Arc*.

At the *fin de siècle*, J. K. Huysmans wrote a notorious, decadent novel, *Là-Bas*, inspired by the excesses of Gilles de Rais; later, Georges Bataille, who was engaged all his life with defining the sacred and the profane, and used pornography to expose social conventions, argued in his edition of the Breton nobleman's trial that his excesses epitomize the power of the aristocracy and the profligacy of chivalry—their extravagant clothes, their butchery out hunting, and their pitiless violence towards the poor whose lands they raided.

Both these writers' imaginings flow into the novel about *La Barbe bleue* and Joan of Arc that Michel Tournier published in 1983, in which he returns to the lurid stories of paedophiliac, satanist carnage committed by Gilles de Rais. He conveys no scepticism over their historical status; for him, the fictional form of the *conte* offers that crystalline translucency through which a more profound truth appears.

Charges of witchcraft were not infrequent in the fifteenth century and posterity usually treats them with utter scepticism, as in the case of Joan of Arc. Historians prefer to examine the context that led to such serious fears, arguing from observation of evidence and the social, political, and perhaps personal tensions it reveals. Yet, running against the grain of ordinary and reasonable scepticism, the guilt of Gilles de Rais has been taken at face value on the basis of the evidence at the trial. It has always seemed to me improbable that so many children—between 80 and 200—could have gone missing without explanation over a period of years without leaving some traces, or causing an outcry from the victims' families, before Gilles was accused and tried. One of the worst riots in Paris, for example, broke out in 1750, when children were regularly going missing. The king Louis XV—or one of his daughters—was suspected of kidnapping them to drink their blood, a remedy that had been prescribed, it was rumoured, by the royal physicians to restore the royal health. No similar riots are recorded in Brittany at the time that Gilles de Rais was accused of the deaths of so many children, and because of this as well as other reasons (his chief prosecutor inherited all his offices and possessions), historians have expressed doubts about his crimes.

The case of Gilles de Rais is particularly interesting because, like the uprising of 1750, it reveals the continual interplay of existing fantasies with historical events. Another obvious problem with identifying Gilles de Rais as *La Barbe bleue* is that Gilles, if he was a mass murderer, chose his victims among little boys: his legend does not depicts him as a serial wife-killer, but rather closer to a classic fairy-tale ogre, snacking in the night on an infant or two until a clever young hero dupes him.

The case of Snow White has also inspired a quest for a historical original. For example, in the exhibition *Treasures of Heaven* at the British Museum (2012), one of the many relics, set in a scintillated jewelled reliquary, remembered the death of St Ludmila, the grandmother of King Wenceslas of the Christmas carol. She's the patron saint of Bohemia and much revered to this day. She was murdered by her mother-in-law, the label went on, who grew jealous of her goodness and beauty and strangled her with her veil.

There have been several bids to identify the authentic model for the Grimms' heroine: in 1994, a German scholar, Eckhard Sander, proposed Margarete von Waldeck (b. 1553), who was possibly poisoned in dynastic scheming of the time. Margarete also grew up in a town (Wildungen) where children went down the copper mines and, Sander continues, were consequently stunted, and taunted as 'poor dwarfs'.

Claims by historians that they have identified Bluebeard or unearthed the first, authentic Snow White reveal a thirst for stable genealogies—something that can never be appeased. Snow White's situation is historical and generic: it encapsulates fundamental dynamics of family life over a *longue durée*, unfortunately. It is reflected in the fury of Venus against Psyche after her son Cupid has fallen in love with her in *The Golden Ass*, for example. Shakespeare dramatizes the conflict in *Cymbeline*, when the Queen—stepmother to the heroine Imogen—schemes against her. In her very first speech, she alludes to 'the slander of most stepmothers' (I.i.85) and hastens to reassure Imogen that she will not act stereotypically. But she attempts to poison her, of course. In *Pericles*, another evil queen orders Marina killed, because she's gifted with more qualities than her own daughter. Shakespeare knows such plots from his historical sources, because the tensions were commonplace, especially in early medieval history when women could occupy positions of power but were always poised precariously, easily unseated by a rival. Like 'Bluebeard', the fairy tale of 'Snow White' does not record a single, appalling crime, but testifies to a structural and endemic conflict in society that was political and social as well as personal, producing many, many instances of similar violence.

The elements are stirred into the pot of story. Occasionally, a *fait divers*, news item or true-life story, does make its way directly into the soup. *The Tales of the Thousand and One Nights* gathers in several incidents reported from history—and transmutes them into fairytale romance. 'The Tale of al-Mutawakkil' (the 10th Caliph, d. 861) and Mahbuba, his beloved concubine, relates how, after a long estrangement, he dreams of her and of their reconciliation; soon after he wakes up, a slave slips him a note; al-Mutawakkil steals into the women's quarters and finds Mahbuba singing; the poem—of her own composition—describes how she saw him come to her in a dream to make peace with her.

Mutual dreaming is one of the distinctive enchantments of the *Nights*, and after this, the lovers are reconciled—until the Caliph's murder. In this story, Mahbuba then pines away and dies, to live forever as a symbol of faithful love. (In historical reality she was handed over to the next ruler, but refused to oblige him, was thrown into prison, and lost to view.)

André Miquel, translator and editor of the *Nights*, has commented that this story discloses rather clearly the warp and weft of history and fantasy in such literature, but it remains unusual in featuring by name individuals who once existed: epics such as *La Chanson de Roland*, or fantastic biographies, such as the Alexander romance, do so as a matter of course, but fairy tales usually bring ordinary mortals centre stage. In the same way as the runaway girl wears a pelican skin in the Spanish version of 'Donkeyskin', so local incidents and memories add colour and point to an existing tale, long after the historical memory of them has faded.

The scholar Catherine Velay-Vallantin has shown how the story of the *Bête de Gevaudan*, a French variation on the

Beast of Dartmoor and other legends, became interwoven with the retellings of 'Red Riding Hood' in provincial France. The *Bête* was a monstrous creature, reputedly a huge wolf, which took the lives of many before it was finally hunted down. The local bishop fulminated against the morals of the community, identifying the Beast as a sure sign from God of their sinfulness, both to bring former Huguenots into line, and to terrorize rural shepherd girls into Christian modesty and decorum: 'This idolatrous and criminal flesh,' he ranted, 'which serves only as a demonic instrument for seducing and condemning souls, should it not be given unto the murderous teeth of the ferocious Beast to tear it to pieces?'

Occasionally, the necessary transformation into fiction does not convince, and the *nouvelle* remains one, failing to crystallize as a *conte*. The Grimms, for example, collected a savage episode in a tale called 'Playing Butchers': 'There once was a father who slaughtered a pig, and his children saw that. In the afternoon, when they began playing, one child said to the other, "you be the little pig, and I'll be the butcher." He then took a shiny knife and slit his little brother's throat.'

The Grimms had found the story in a Berlin newspaper edited by the Romantic writer Heinrich von Kleist, so it hardly had authentic *Volk* credentials, except as an urban myth; it does have analogues in folklore elsewhere, but its pitilessness aroused shock and horror in the first readers of *Children's and Household Tales*, and the Grimms came under pressure to drop it. They did so in later editions of their collection. But Wilhelm protested that it taught children the all-important distinction between playing make-believe and real life. He saw the wisdom in the tales as cautionary as well as consolatory.

Common Bonds

On the whole, though, the historical reality that can be excavated from fairy tales does not carry the memory of extreme horrors, specific tragedies, or individuals, but rather dramatizes ordinary circumstances, daily sufferings, needs, desires—and dangers, especially of dying young. Rather than seek for a particular vicious individual behind a fairy-tale figure, or for a specific event, thinking of the stories as responses to *generic* human experience yields far greater results. The story of Bluebeard touches upon areas of acute anxiety—about male sexuality in general and in extremis; about the rights of husbands—and the rights of wives; about money (Bluebeard is always vastly wealthy); about foreigners and Orientals; about the delinquency of curiosity and women's special propensity to be curious. The deaths of his wives one after another may offer a historical memory of the toll of childbirth.

Also, it is important to realize that the traffic does not only go one way, the fairy tale taking colour from real life. Real life is understood in the light of the stories, too. That pre-Revolutionary Parisian violence was suffused with a fairytale dread of child-guzzling ogres who came straight from the pages of 'Jack and the Beanstalk' or 'Hop o'My Thumb' or, one could say, the collective imaginary.

And fantasy often exercises a stronger pull than reality: Gilles de Rais is far more compelling cast as a fairytale monster bridegroom than he is as a victim of feudal and ecclesiastical ambition in medieval France.

In one sense the nightmare of Bluebeard overlaps with the terrors of penny dreadfuls and tabloid journalism about Jack the Ripper and other extreme, specific horrors. In another sense, however, the murderer bridegroom and his persistent presence in the tales symbolize more general grounds of acute anxiety. The voyeuristic violence has a moral dimension, too; what is the pleasure for the reader (and the writer) of the bloody chamber?

'Bluebeard', 'Beauty and the Beast', and many other fairy tales about monster bridegrooms appear to focus on the villain, the male protagonist. But they are as entangled with the bride and with questions of female desire as they are with male drives. Bluebeard's afterlife in literature and other media divides sharply along gender lines: male writers see themselves in the role, with varying degrees of self-scrutiny and complacency, whereas for women, the Bluebeard figure often embodies contradictory feelings about male sexuality, and consequently presents a challenge, a challenge they meet in a variety of ways. The fascination and the repulsion that beast bridegrooms provoke in women turns such stories into explorations of female sexuality, and this strand has become one of the powerful attractions of the whole genre. Bluebeard typifies the principal male antagonist in the sex wars, an enemy, a sadist, and a rapist—who can also be irresistibly alluring.

His house, his castle, his forbidden chamber become synonymous with forbidden knowledge: when the heroine of

Angela Carter's variation on the fairy tale first sees the place where she is being taken:

> And, ah! his castle. The faery solitude of the place; with its turrets of misty blue, its courtyard, its spiked gate, his castle that lay on the very bosom of the sea with seabirds mewing about its attics, the casements opening on to the green and purple, evanescent departures of the ocean, cut off by the tide from land for half a day . . . that castle, at home neither on the land nor on the water, a mysterious, amphibious place, contravening the materiality of both earth and the waves, with the melancholy of a mermaiden who perches on her rock and waits, endlessly, for a lover who had drowned far away, long ago. That lovely, sad, sea-siren of a place!

This enchanted fortress conceals a torture chamber.

The bride is initiated into erotic pleasure by this Blue-beard, but rescued, in a rightly celebrated, exuberant twist at the end of the story, by the arrival of her sharp-shooting mother: 'You never saw such a wild thing as my mother, her hat seized by the winds and blown out to sea so that her hair was her white mane, her black lisle legs exposed to the thigh, her skirts tucked round her waist, one hand on the reins of the rearing horse while the other clasped my father's service revolver and . . .'.

This vision owes something to the bewitched Highland crew, Cutty Sark and her ilk, whom Carter knew from her Highlander granny.

The heroine of Geneviève Breillat's low-budget, art house movie *Barbe-bleue* (2009) also gets the better of her rich, obese, doting husband; this perverse rendering by a woman director, who has been censured for earlier pornographic work, deliberately evokes children's pop-up story books in design and narration, and ends with a tableau of the bride contemplating Bluebeard's head on a platter, a victorious Salome with the head of John the Baptist. This revenge eludes the protagonist of E. L. James's sado-masochist sensation, *Fifty Shades of Grey*; in this case, the female author chooses to let Bluebeard have his way.

In the twenty-first century, the politics of the bedchamber communicate a different perspective on the dangers that sex presents to a young woman.

Heroic Optimism

The nesting places of the storyteller, Walter Benjamin pointed out, are in the loom shed and at the spinning wheel, in the fulling barn and the kitchen when doing tedious, repetitive tasks—shelling peas in readiness for storing, sorting pulses for bagging, bottling and preserving. Stories were told to alleviate harsh labour and endless drudgery—and they were passed between generations—by the voice of experience, filled with the laughter of defiance, the hope of just deserts.

For this reason, many readers have found in fairy tales a powerful 'consolatory fable' for the sufferings that ordinary people went through, and the proof of the emancipatory spirit of the oppressed in action. Idealists, reformers, self-styled prophets and utopians, are especially attracted to the form, and it is significant how many writers borrowed the conventions of fairy tales to campaign for social reforms: some, such as Charles Kingsley, Christina Rossetti, and

C. S. Lewis, were devout Christians; others, from John Ruskin to Frank L. Baum, Antonio Gramsci to Philip Pullman, envision alternative societies, often organized along socialist lines. J. K. Rowling's political commitment to the cause of single mothers, for example, and her strong egalitarian feelings, are entirely of a piece with forerunners in the world of the expanded fairytale form.

The happy ending, that defining dynamic of fairy tales, follows from their relation to reality. Ordinary misery and its causes are the stories' chief concern. But writers—and storytellers—address their topics with craft, and it is often more compelling to translate experience through metaphor and fantasy than to put it plainly. As C. S. Lewis wrote in the title of one of his essays, 'Sometimes Fairy Stories May Say Best What's To Be Said'.

Even a writer as dreamy (and privileged) as the German Romantic Novalis defined the form as a way of thinking up a way out: 'A *true fairytale* must also be a *prophetic account of things*—an ideal account—an absolutely necessary account. A true writer of fairy tales sees into the future.'

The stories face up to the inadmissible facts of reality and promise deliverance. This honest harshness combined with the wishful hoping has helped them to last. If literature is a place we go to, in Seamus Heaney's words, 'to be forwarded within ourselves' then fairy tales form an important part of it. If literature gives 'an experience that is like foreknowledge of certain things which we already seem to be remembering', fairy tales offer enigmatic, terrifying images of what the prospects are, of the darkest horrors life may bring. Yet the stories usually imagine ways of opposing this

95

state of affairs, or at worst, of having revenge on those who inflict suffering, of turning the status quo upside down, as well as defeating the natural course of events; they dream of reprisals, and they sketch alternative plot lines. They are messages of hope arising from desperate yet ordinary situations.

5

Childish Things

Pictures & Conversations

> Each picture told a story...as interesting as the tales
> Bessie sometimes narrated on winter evenings...and
> when, having brought her ironing-table to the nursery
> hearth, she allowed us to sit about it, and...fed our
> eager attention with passages of love and adventure
> taken from old fairy tales and other ballads...
>
> With Bewick on my knee, I was then happy: happy
> at least in my way.
>
> Charlotte Brontë, *Jane Eyre*

Jane Eyre is the first little girl—or, if not the first, the most
celebrated—to tell us her story in a novel in the first person;
she is 10 years old, and taking refuge from the bullying of
her cousin by hiding away in a red alcove and losing herself
in a picture book.

A forerunner of Alice in Wonderland in the ranks of
fictional child protagonists, and the heroine of a novel that
is shot through with the vivid colours, grotesqueness,
and cruelty of romances and fairy tales, the young Jane is

mind-voyaging as she reads, a pastime much disapproved by her vicious foster-family (so like a fairy tale). But Thomas Bewick's *History of British Birds* in her lap is twinned, in the passage, with memories of her beloved nurse Bessie telling tales while she was ironing, and this collocation, of real birds in pictures and remembered stories told aloud, foreshadows the scene of storytelling that has now become the dominant advice to parents: reading to a small child with a picture book open and shared between them.

This is a familiar image of good parenting, but it is formed by modern ideas about children, the value of stories, and the truth of the imagination.

Yet in 1855, when Charlotte Brontë died, fairy tales were not yet routinely published with illustrations. Woodcuts of birds by Thomas Bewick, the creator of beguiling pastoral vignettes, belong to enlightened, humanist pedagogy which urged that young minds explore phenomena empirically, according to reason. John Locke and Jean-Jacques Rousseau were opposed to fancy (children had enough of that naturally), although they agreed with the Romantics when they too observed nature, and saw 'a world in a grain of sand | And a heaven in a wild flower'.

The illustrated book is an essential dynamic in the history of fairy tale, for since the nineteenth century the stories have been principally transmitted through visual storytelling—on stage and screen as well as from the page. At the beginning of *Through the Looking Glass*, Alice's creator specifically diagnoses one of the drawbacks of books for a child, when she reacts with impatience at her sister reading a book. Alice wants to know what's in it, but when she peeps at it she thinks to herself, with a touch of that sturdy scepticism that helps her survive the ordeals of Wonderland, 'What is the use of a book without pictures or conversations?'

When Lewis Carroll dedicated *Through the Looking Glass* to Alice Liddell, he looked back at that golden afternoon when he first made up the story to amuse her and her siblings:

> The magic words shall hold thee fast:
> Thou shalt not heed the raving blast...
> It shall not touch, with breath of bale,
> The pleasance of our fairy tale.

Although few would agree to apply the term to the Alice books today, they are the supreme success of a new kind of book, one with a crucial role to play in the unfolding history of the magic or wonder tale.

When the first Alice book appeared in 1869, illustrated journals and picture books were among the most innovatory, inspired, and idiosyncratic currents of British culture. From the start of his conception, the Reverend Charles Dodgson (Lewis Carroll) determined that his story would have pictures, and he took his cue from the success of the Grimms in their first English appearance, which was illustrated by George Cruikshank, one of the Punch stable of cartoonists. John Tenniel was another and, in a momentous move for the fortunes of Alice, Carroll showed him his own preparatory drawings and asked him to improve on them (see Figure 9).

Pictures imprint more strongly than words: who ever forgets the illustrations that first rose from the pages of a book in childhood—of Alice swimming in a pool of her own tears?

and
imm
those
blue
whic
with
-ed,
a lon
takin
notic
of ar

time
at ea
silen

the caterpillar took the hookah out
mouth, and languidly addressed her

Figure 9 'Who are *you*?', the Caterpillar asks, but Alice doesn't quite know. From Lewis Carroll's manuscript copy of *Alice's Adventures Under Ground*, 1862–4.

I remember how twisting branches and twiggy knobbly fingers seemed to stick out to grab me from a gnarled tree with a pointed, gleefully greedy face. The picture—by Arthur Rackham—frightened me terribly and gave me ideas about woods that I never would have had by myself, since I lived in a polite suburb of a city where forests were a remote and exotic thought (see Figure 3). I can bring up in my mind's eye images from books I had as a child of moments that artists crystallized: the prince spurting blood as he's caught by the thorns around Sleeping Beauty's castle, Hansel and Gretel holding hands as they look for the trail of breadcrumbs in the forest, only to find that the birds have eaten them.

The Arabian Nights or Basile's *Pentameron* had not implied a child audience, and the stories are raunchy and explicit in ways that would not meet the conditions of the nine o'clock watershed. Perrault's *Contes* and Grimms' *Tales* included children in their sights, but not exclusively. The first chapbooks did not single out child readers, but from the early nineteenth century, writers, collectors, editors, re-tellers, and publishers began aiming specifically at the young. How did the change happen, from Shakespeare's dramas and the Grimm Brothers' collection to this modern focus on fairy tales as a necessary but tricky tool in child development?

The rejection of fairy tales by critics such as Locke and Rousseau was moved by generally enlightened principles and rational ideals: bogeymen were traditionally used by nurses and parents to frighten children into good behaviour and the stories were full of scare figures—ogres, witches, monsters. The motifs of child-snatchers like the Sandman and witches were invoked as threats. Excitable young people were prone to nightmares, and adults should not over-excite them. Women were targets of these criticisms, bracketed with children on account of their work in child-raising, but also because they were seen as intellectually susceptible to foolish fantasies, too. The imagined popular—and foreign—origin of so many fairy tales also aroused condemnation among the educated. For example, when the *Arabian Nights* first appeared in English, Lord Shaftesbury protested against the enthusiasm of their reception: '[the tales] excite in them a passion for a mysterious Race of black Enchanters: such as of old were said to creep into Houses, and lead captive silly Women.'

Literary historians have consequently perceived a strong opposition between realistic fiction on the one hand and fantasy on the other, and made much of the resistance among educationalists to fairy tale, unless doctored to promote virtue. The rise of the novel of manners, of naturalistic representations in fiction and of a commitment to contemporary social settings (Auden's 'feigned histories') accompanied a decline of esteem for fabulist forms and fantasy conventions. What Lewis calls the realism of presentation was admired, to the disadvantage of magic and enchantment. Fairy tales had however always had detractors, even among those who were writig them. Perrault was quick to present his tales as mere *sornettes* (trifles) and the earliest readers of the *Nights*, including one of their greatest imitators, Anthony Hamilton, also scoffed at the stories as old wives' tales. Nonsense had its place, in the playground and the nursery; Richard Dawkins is only the latest critic to proclaim that putting fantasy behind one is part of growing up.

But children did not and do not turn to books for witty descriptions of manners and morals in the Pump Room at Bath. It needs no prior experience, by contrast, for the events recounted in fairy tales to make a child laugh or shiver spontaneously. Sometimes, in fact often, a child is the hero or heroine, so identification can be immediate. And children could be allowed to believe in magic and metamorphosis, though their elders had to put away such childish things, and believe only in the wonders of the Bible.

Caroline Sumpter, in her excellent book on the Victorian press, has however modified this traditional contrast in a most interesting way. She discusses how popular journalistic media in the eighteenth century had already adopted 'the Fairy Way of writing', and that fairy tales began circulating in the new periodicals: the *Arabian Nights* were serialized over several months to huge excitement—and imitation; printers like John Newbery began to re-tell home-grown legends and tales for child readers; and, from the heartlands of Romanticism, Mary Jane Clairmont, the second wife of William Godwin, and Mary Shelley's stepmother, had the idea of bringing out French fairy tales for children in an attempt to make some much needed money for the family (she has not been given her due by biographers, in my view).

The Romantic vision of childhood led to the triumph of the imagination, but also to the belief that the faculty of make-believe was a child's special privilege—J. M. Barrie's Peter Pan has escaped what Wordsworth called 'the shades of the prison house'. Grown-ups yearned to regain that paradise—the land of the lost boys—and evoking this secondary world became a powerful spur to new fairytale fictions. These were often dreams of young protagonists putting warped adult society to rights: Alice is a supreme example, a little girl who, like the little boy in Andersen's 'The Emperor's New Clothes', questions adult folly. Some children in Victorian fairy tales are bad seeds, but most of them hold up ideals for a better world.

So fairy tale, while aimed especially at modern children, hovered as a form of literature between them and adults; it was, in many senses, always a crossover form of quite exceptional fertility, efflorescing into works by Hans Andersen, George MacDonald, E. Nesbit, Diana Wynne-Jones, and Neil Gaiman. The adult reader has never quit the scene: as parents, as grandparents, as teachers, as babysitters, we have continued to read and watch fairy tales alongside the young, simply for our own pleasure. Yet the implied childish angle of view shapes the characters and their transformations in the story. Pictures are crucial to the appeal made to the ideal child reader and, on the whole, the role of artists who helped create fairy tales has been neglected. Andrew Lang's huge success with the *Fairy Books* owes a great deal to the richly detailed Pre-Raphaelite wood engravings by H. J. Ford, with their elongated, graceful, and impossibly long-haired heroines in medieval jewels and costumes. Artists such as Gustave Doré, Arthur Rackham, Edmund Dulac, Walter Crane, Lotte Reiniger, and Walt Disney have also defined the feel and flavour of the genre as much as the writers they have visualized for the page and the screen; they have also conducted a conversation among themselves, which continues: Edward Scissorhands could have been drawn by Rackham and neither artist's work would look the way it does without Reiniger (see Figures 3, 12, 13, and 15).

Child Readers: The Story Nook and the Niche Market

In the very first printed fairy tales (Perrault in English chapbooks), the stories were illustrated with crude but pointed woodcuts: Jack tiny beside the enormous head of the giant, Bluebeard's wife hauled by her hair, with the brothers tiny figures at full tilt in the background. But printing technology would soon make books with pictures one of the most exciting and successful ventures of the nineteenth century, and fairy tales began to be produced deliberately to appeal to an audience of young readers. Light-heartedness, humour, and a certain nonchalance helped adapt the matter of fairy tale to the new child audience. Fairy tales shifted to a comic register—'pills for melancholy'. It is significant that when the Grimms were first translated and published in English by Edgar Taylor in 1823, Cruikshank set a mood of jolly good fun, or silly, whacky nonsense, in the spirit of nursery rhymes such as the story of 'Old Dame Trot and her Marvellous Cat'.

Cruikshank's frontispieces show a comical little grandpa roaring with laughter and kicking up his heels, and a venerable granny or Mother Goose gathering a rapt clutch of little ones around her knees.

In this way the Victorians nudged the material into the nursery. Cruikshank's pictures draw us—the readers—into the scene of storytelling, just as the images of Old Mother Goose and Mother Bunch did in other books of fairy tales. His illustrations for the two volumes of Edgar Taylor's *German Popular Stories* set a trend not only in this country but all over the world, because the tales were definitively presented for the entertainment of little ones, and amended and cut accordingly, the terrors defused by the artist's genial caricatures of the ogres and other adversaries. The emphasis falls on the high spirits of the heroes and heroines, not on the ghastly ordeals they suffer. Cruikshank's pictures are gay in the old sense: they give us sweet-faced heroines, plucky lads, and dancing elves. The magic animals are comical and endearing, the giants are goofy, their rage absurd and easily managed; and he does not illustrate the cruellest tales like 'Snow White' or 'The Juniper Tree' (see Figure 10).

The flow of stories began to form a new watershed in the territory of narrative, built of books made with children in mind, lavishly illustrated to increase their appeal. So successful was the attempt that copies of early children's fairy-tale books have become scarce—especially copies that haven't been damaged, the villain's face scribbled over, the monster torn out. But survivors from their readers' tough love spread a feast of wit and colour: harlequinades and concertinas, toy books like miniature theatres, pop-ups and sliding tabs bring the familiar plots to life with exuberant resourcefulness. These possibilities, growing more and more diverse through the nineteenth century, as brilliant twists to reproduction and printing technologies were developed, wrought a major change in the history of fairy tales.

Later, after Taylor's edition proved such a success, Cruik-shank made his own selection for a book called *The Fairy Library*, which came out in 1853–4; he tempered the tales and added others. His family was all too familiar with Gin Lane, and Cruikshank was an ardent campaigner against

Figure 10 Devices of enchantment: 'Then the fox stretched out its tail again, and away they went...'. 'The Golden Bird' by the Brothers Grimm, illustrated by George Cruikshank, 1825-6.

drink, the ravager of so many. In his version of 'Cinderella', the fountains flow with lemonade at her wedding.

Dickens instantly responded with a furious protest at his friend's bowdlerization, as he saw it. He rose to the defence of the tales' truth to life in an article called 'Frauds on the

Fairies': 'the little books [themselves], nurseries of fancy as they are, should be preserved. To preserve them in their usefulness, they must be as much preserved in their simplicity, and purity, and innocent extravagance, as if they were actual fact. Whoever alters them to suit his own opinions, whatever they are, is guilty, to our thinking, of an act of presumption, and appropriates to himself what does not belong to him.'

But Dickens was not heard. After the transformation of the Grimms had taken place, many other fairytale collections were similarly de-fanged. The perception of them was startlingly mild, and indeed Dickens, that fierce champion of unadulterated fairy tales, seems to be unaware of 'The Juniper Tree' or even 'Snow White' when he declares: 'It would be hard to estimate the amount of gentleness and mercy that has made its way among us through these slight channels. Forbearance, courtesy, consideration for poor and aged, kind treatment of animals, love of nature, abhorrence of tyranny and brute force—many such good things have been first nourished in the child's heart by this powerful aid.'

The age of the stories' heroes and heroines begins to grow younger and younger alongside their readers. Dickens and Andersen both sought popular success by performing their stories live, often adding pictures: Dickens was a brilliant mimic and used a magic lantern; Andersen was a wizard at making paper cut-out figures.

Hans Christian Andersen is the most significant original creator of fairy tales of the Victorian period, when the genre settled as suitable children's fare. He drew inspiration from his family—his travelling father (a fisherman), his fanciful grandmother, and his mother, a washerwoman on the margins of respectability. But he never fully admitted his indebtedness to them—Andersen's vanity and snobbery are legendary. He was not however working alone as a literary innovator, either, and it was a friend and mentor who, aware of the literary fashions in Germany, encouraged the young writer to leave off his plodding epics and try his hand at wonder. Like Dickens and unlike the Grimms, Andersen consciously operated as an original author, and altered, expanded, and embroidered his source material, ranging from melodrama to jokiness, and putting an unmistakable stamp of his own: maudlin, even morbid stories like 'The Little Mermaid' and 'The Little Match Girl', and thrilling, peculiar adventures, like 'The Tinder Box' and 'The Shadow', are rightly considered classics.

The fairy way of writing, packaged and pictured for younger readers, became a mode of communicating moral values, political dreams, and even scientific knowledge. It provided Victorian, Edwardian, and, later, contemporary writers with a form through which they could express their experiences and ideals. Fairy tales settled into the canon of childhood education, and became recommended reading while growing up because they stimulate the mind's capacity to visualize and follow a story, because they convey real conditions and teach wisdom in dealing with life's experiences, especially the passage through adolescence. With these writers a golden age of writing for children began; the remarkable flowering of the form, especially in Britain, exhibits features consciously adapted from Perrault, Grimm, and the *Arabian Nights*; it exploits the possibilities of the wonders which fairytale inventors had naturalized in the landscape of the imagination.

Darkness Rising: Fairy Tale and Contemporary Art

The Grimms have been illustrated in a thousand ways by a multitude of artists since Cruikshank, and the tone is darkening, in the work of artists like Paula Rego who embrace the graphic tradition and its skills (see Figure 7). In 1969 the artist David Hockney chose six fairy tales by the Brothers Grimm and illustrated them with intense, spare, spiky etchings. The tiny leather-bound book is a classic of visual storytelling; it was an immediate huge success, considered a breakthrough in print-making, a sign of Sixties energy and swinging London; its thirty-nine images constantly tour the world and continue to reappear in the illustrations and designs of other books, films, and operas.

Three of the stories Hockney chose are very familiar: 'Rapunzel', 'Rumpelstiltskin', and 'The Boy Who Left Home to Learn Fear'. But he also turned his extraordinary graphic imagination to several barely known tales: 'The Little Sea Hare', 'Old Rinkrank', 'Fundevogel', and 'The Riddle Princess'. The etchings are all subtle and mordant and deadpan like the best of Grimm; they're adventurous technically with delicate stipplings and cross-hatchings, and they're constantly surprising: even after fifty years, they turn the tales into hooked sensors that catch at the mind with their fine quavery lines and then sink in thornily, but pleasurably: the princess perched at the top of her slender tower in her glass hexagon,

Figure 11 How to hide from a cruel princess: 'The fish swallowed the boy and dived to the bottom of the lake.' David Hockney, 'The Boy Hidden in a Fish', from 'The Little Sea Hare', in *Six Fairy Tales from the Brothers Grimm*, 1969.

and baby Rapunzel sitting in the lap of Mother Gothel—every inch the Virgin Mary (except that she has a beard)—or the hero crouching and hidden inside the fish (Figure 11).

The tale of 'Fundevogel' (Foundling Bird)—a miniature in the Grimm collection—brought out the virtuoso in Hockney. The pot in which Foundling Bird is going to be thrown is winking with bubbles of water on the boil; it looks utterly ordinary, but at the same time brimming with poisonous menace. This is the true spirit of the uncanny: the banal holds terrible secrets. Turn the page and the cook in profile holds up her spoon like a cudgel. Later, Hockney does the children's transformations as they flee her: the rose and the church and the lake...each of them intensely filled with presence, even though the book in which they appear is smaller than a playing card.

That is the way fairy tales should be: like the splinter from the spindle, they can enter you and remain for a hundred years of dreams. Hockney's album, *Six Fairy Tales*, helped pluck the Grimms out of the Victorian age, and made them our contemporaries, crossing over from the nursery back again to the grown-ups as the brothers had intended from the start.

Two centuries later, fairy tales, especially the Brothers Grimm variety, no longer appear such innocent amusement.

6

On the Couch

House-Training the Id

The Old Man of the Earth stooped over the floor of the
cave, raised a huge stone from it, and left it leaning. It
disclosed a great hole that went plumb-down.
'That is the way,' he said.
'But there are no stairs.'
'You must throw yourself in. There is no other way.'

George MacDonald, *The Golden Key*

In 1976, Bruno Bettelheim, a psychoanalyst who had survived
imprisonment as a child in Dachau and Buchenwald, published one of the most influential studies of fairy tales ever
written, *The Uses of Enchantment*. It first appeared in the *New
Yorker* magazine, gaining it a far wider readership than psychoanalytical scholarship usually commands, even in the
island of Manhattan, and its line of argument was powerfully
expressed and very persuasive. It is still the best-known study of
fairy tale, though it was and remains controversial and flawed.

That fairy tales are cast in a language of the psyche, with
the forests and palaces, snow, glass, and apples symbolizing

deeper, concealed truths, has become widely accepted; psychoanalytical methods provide entry into the stories' meanings, and, like the hotel maid's key, can open every door, including those that lead to forbidden chambers, the dark corners of humankind in general as well as the secrets of a particular individual. Fairy tales mean far more than the plots they unfold; they resemble dreams, which unfold as enigmas but can be deciphered. The scholar Maria Tatar has noted: 'Fairy tales are still arguably the most powerfully formative tales of childhood and permeate mass media for children and adults...The staying power of these stories, their widespread and enduring popularity, suggests that they must be addressing issues that have a significant social function—whether critical, conservative, compensatory, or therapeutic...Fairy tales register an effort on the part of both women and men to develop maps for coping with personal anxieties, family conflicts, social fictions, and the myriad frustrations of everyday life.'

Charles Perrault added *moralités* to make the lessons of his tales clear, rounding off his 'Little Red Riding Hood' with sly patter about how disobeying Mother will end in tears, and that wolves can be hairy on the inside, smooth-tongued seducers, who inveigle young girls into their bedchambers and ruin them. 'These young men are the most dangerous wolves of all...'.

His tongue-in-cheek morality sets the scene for 'Red Riding Hood' (Figure 12) as a fairy tale of initiation, an allegory of carnal knowledge and social prohibitions, about innocent girlhood on the threshold of maturity, with the trackless forest standing in for the dangerous world, the predator for

Figure 12 'There are real wolves ... with enormous teeth ... but also wolves who ... pay young girls the most flattering attentions ...'. Gustave Doré, 'Red Riding Hood', 1883.

the seducer, the abuser of innocence. The view has since taken on a deep psychological meaning.

Bettelheim was following Freud in turning to fairy tales, for while the founder of psychoanalysis chiefly drew on myth for his theories, he also invoked fairy tales in order to decipher the language of the unconscious and identify plots that illuminate the imperatives of desire—the drives to love and death. Like so many other children, Sigmund Freud grew up with the tales of the Brothers Grimm, and their themes and symbols offered him a rich and useful lexicon to understand varieties of behaviour and vagaries of fortune. His interest is however a paradox, because fairy tales hardly brush ideas about individual personality or motive, and they never enquire into inner processes. The characters do what they do without question—from themselves or from us.

The novelist A. S. Byatt, who has revisioned mermaid tales as well as Norse sagas, writes, 'Their world is full of narrative energy, but there are things they don't do. They don't analyse feelings.' Philip Pullman goes further:

> There is no psychology in a fairy tale. The characters have little interior life; their motives are clear and obvious. If people are good, they are good, and if bad, they're bad...The tremors and mysteries of human awareness, the whispers of memory, the promptings of half-understood regret or doubt or desire that are so much part of the subject matter of the modern novel are absent entirely.
>
> One might almost say that the characters in a fairy tale are not actually conscious.

Yet fairytale narratives are dream-like; they're disjointed, brilliantly coloured, they overlook rational cause and effect, they stage outlandish scenes of sex and violence, and they make abrupt transitions without rhyme or reason. They also contain significant repetitions and recurrent symbols. For Freud dreams concealed 'a certain secret quality of your being which it is hard to follow...but in the deepest sense this is not in the least so; indeed, it cannot be so at all—for it is always the same man, whether he is awake or dreaming'.

The same can be said about fairy tales, projected on to a collective psyche across time. Freud also saw them as rubble from a primitive stage of humanity, which remains chaotically strewn about during infantile development: phylogenesis (development of the species) was recapitulated in the growth of each individual from infant to adult (ontogenesis). Fairy tales, like dreams, used a vernacular of motifs that could disclose latent and hitherto unacknowledged preoccupations and desires. He gives as his example Hans Andersen's story, 'The Emperor's New Clothes'. The end, when the emperor walks out naked in procession before the whole town, is just like a common dream—when you find yourself in public without any clothes on. 'It is in this human content that our interests lie', he writes in 1913, and five years later, in his famous analysis of the Wolf Man (1918), he recognizes his patient's terrors as the predator in 'The Wolf and the Seven Young Kids' and 'Little Red Riding Hood', in which the animal embodies a traumatic childhood encounter.

Freud also explores, more illuminatingly, one pre-eminent quality of fairy tales and their dream-like atmosphere. He called it the *Unheimlich* (literally, the unhomely), and it

117

BOX 4 *Sibling Rivalry v. Sibling Love*
....

Freud's method of interpretation looked for latent significance of a story's symbols: in 'The Theme of the Three Caskets', he analyses the riddle test that Portia's father set her suitors in *The Merchant of Venice*, and fastens on the figure of the youngest sister, the selfless, put-upon child, who is ultimately vindicated. He says she represents Death, the last of the three faces of the Mother, when she takes you in her arms and you are laid in earth. She is the most 'inexorable of the Fates', he adds, and he chooses for his example the Grimms' fairy tale 'The Twelve Brothers'.

Twelve sons are born to a king and queen. The king then swears that if a girl is born, all the boys will have to die. The decree seems a bit extreme, but this is one of those baffling horrific oracles that drive fairytale plots. The power of it lies in its ineluctability: nobody asks why things should be so.

The queen hides her sons deep in a forest, and they swear they will kill any girl they meet.

Their sister grows up with a golden star on her forehead, in oblivion of their existence, until one day she sees her mother hanging out twelve shirts on the washing line. When she asks whose they might be, her mother shows her the twelve coffins already prepared for the boys.

This heroine is another brave heart from fairy tale, selfless and good. She's prepared to die to save her brothers, and she sets out with the shirts to find them.

The story takes another dramatic turn when, after she has discovered them deep in the forest, she picks lilies to give them, and they're instantly turned into ravens. It then becomes her task to save them—and the condition for doing this is silence. She must not speak for seven years.

Terrible ordeals follow...she is condemned for a witch and tied to a stake and the fire lit...but the ravens fly down and save her in the nick of time.

For Freud, her muteness makes her the representation of Death itself, the goddess of death. He comments: 'Such a displacement will surprise us least of all in relation to the goddess of death, since in modern versions and representations, which these stories would thus anticipate, Death itself is nothing other than a dead man.'

Freud's insights are often poetic, but his identification of the Grimms' mute heroine with the goddess of death might strike us as having little to do with an exciting, mysterious fairy tale about infanticide, bird metamorphosis, and a brave girl rescuing twelve young men.

When I was young this was one of my favourite stories and I did not see its heroine as standing for Death, rather she struck me as proving the strength of love that can exist between siblings, not only lovers.

has been influentially translated in English as 'the Uncanny'. 'Unhomely' catches better the way reality is transfigured into weirdness in the stories, how they act as a peculiar looking-glass into family relations or bare survival.

The Uncanny (1919) explores a terrifying bogeyman figure from German folklore: 'He [the Sandman] is a wicked man who comes when children won't go to bed, and throws handfuls of sand into their eyes so that they jump out of their heads all bleeding. Then he puts the eyes in a sack and carries them off to the half-moon to feed his children. They sit up there in their nest and their beaks are hooked like owls' beaks, and they use them to peck up the eyes of the naughty little boys and girls.'

Freud was reading *The Sandman*, a turbulent Gothic tale by E. T. A. Hoffmann, a haunted and self-destructive writer and composer who drew on popular folklore—fears, superstitions, and stories—for his motifs, but wrought highly original fictions from his sources. In the course of an intensive close reading of Hoffmann's original, Freud gives a master class in the symbolic interpretation of fairy tales. As in dreams, the story condenses fears and repressed desires, and in order to decode them, the series of substitutions and displacements must be unpicked. The Freudian Uncanny does not arise from lurking monsters or witches or other fantasy threats from fairy tale, but is primarily an effect of profound disturbance sparked by something familiar, that is homely, which awakens a repressed memory of forbidden desire or trauma: 'something which ought to have remained hidden but has come to light'. The forest, so bright with dancing sunbeams and fresh flowers, seems homely, but its uncanny ominousness grows as it tempts the little girl off the path. Jack Zipes observes that the secondary world of fairy tale is uncanny *per se* because it 'involves dislocating the reader from his/her familiar setting and then identifying with the dislocated protagonist so that a quest for the *Heimische* or real home can begin.'

Among Freud's dramatis personae the Sandman figures as another tyrant father, and his scary offspring carry the threat that another child—a sibling—might be loved more, while the gruesome putting out of the nestlings' eyes stands for the terror of castration.

The Uncanny also arises, Freud discusses, when the dead return or something inert gives a sudden sign of life—when a skeleton dances or a doll gets up and walks towards you, singing, as the automaton Olympia does in Hoffmann's story—and it's released by unexpected animation, that fundamental feature of magic, the catalyst of the frisson delivered by many illustrations as well as narratives. But the psychoanalytical school of interpretation is not content to leave the effects of articulate body parts—skulls, a horse's head, a severed finger—to simple biological responses to threats. Rather, the shivery effects of the Uncanny, writes Freud, are produced by Oedipal desire and castration anxiety. Eros and Thanatos, oral fixation, Oedipal conflicts and their corollaries—castration anxiety and sibling rivalry, penis envy, repression—the whole gamut of Freudian concepts unfolds in the later explorations of Bettelheim and others.

Freud did not in fact write a great deal about fairy tales, but his large shadow falls aslant Bettelheim's famous book, in which he declares himself the champion of fairy tales as useful educational, emotional, and ethical instruments for helping a child pass through the anxieties and guilt and confusion of infancy and adolescence. He disregards historical changes and contexts, including his own frame of reference and point of departure, and treats his selected tales (principally Grimm) as a book of life written in cipher about everyman, everywoman, and everychild.

The Abuses of Enchantment

Bettelheim took three decisive steps: he declared, first, that fairy tales arise in the unconscious, encode universal human experiences, especially from infancy to adolescence, and offer adults as well as children a blueprint for understanding the feelings and problems of growing up. Sexual symbolism pervades the stories, in a form that communicates states of maturity and helps adjust to them. Secondly, he affirmed that analysing the tales as if they were an individual's dreams can uncover the latent material buried under the narrative about the development of a person— their 'maturation' from childhood to adulthood in relation to family members and objects of desire.

For example, he comments on 'Red Riding Hood':

> All through 'Little Red Cap', in the title as in the girl's name, the emphasis is on the color red, which she openly wears. Red is the color symbolizing violent emotions, very much including sexual ones. The red velvet cap given by Grandmother to Little Red Cap thus can be viewed as a symbol of a premature transfer of sexual attractiveness, which is further accentuated by the grandmother's being old and sick, too weak even to open a door . . . Little Red Cap's danger is her budding sexuality, for which she is not yet emotionally mature enough.

And again, about Cinderella's slipper, he writes:

> However Cinderella may have felt about dwelling among the ashes, she knew that a person who lives thus appears to others as being dirty and uncouth. There are females who feel this way about their sexuality, and others who fear that males feel this way about it. That is why Cinderella made sure that the prince saw her in this state also before he chose her. By handing her the slipper to put her foot into, the prince symbolically expresses that he accepts her the way she is, dirty and degraded.

Thirdly, and most importantly, Bettelheim maintained that the chilly brutality and bloodthirsty vengeance of Grimm fairy tales are ultimately good for children. They can project themselves into the plots, which then provide an outlet for the feelings of hostility and rage they have towards their parents and their siblings—enchantments can be used to overcome the ravages of the Oedipus complex.

The psychoanalytical theory that Bettelheim applied most resonantly to Grimms' *Tales* is known as splitting. Splitting assumes Freud's theory, which he called 'the family romance', that children often fantasize their parents are impostors, and that they have been stolen by them from a far better, kinder, richer, grander family.

Bettelheim sees fairy tales expressing

> the child's hopeful expectation that one day, by chance or design, the real parent will appear and the child will be elevated into his rightful exalted state and live happily ever after.

> These fantasies are helpful; they permit the child to feel really angry at the . . . false parent without guilt.

The evil stepmother comes to embody all the sides of a mother that the children kick against, while the good mother, whom they love and who loves them, remains untouched by their angry, rebellious feelings, and the turmoil of their Oedipal desires (see Figures 1 and 16). When the wicked queen is made to put on red-hot shoes and dance till she drops down dead, she absorbs all the bad feelings children may have, especially towards their mother, and so their guilt and misery are alleviated, and they can exult in the just punishment of their foe. Through such splitting, the end of the Grimms' 'Snow White' becomes therapeutic, not gloating or cruel.

Apart from the universalist assumptions about society, the family, and male–female relations, which make him overlook cultural differences over time, this tolerance, even enthusiasm, for cruelty has led to Bettelheim's book coming under attack.

His own horrific ordeals in the camps had brutalized him, his detractors argue. His career as a doctor included harsh treatment of his patients, it has been further alleged, and his views about the value of violence in imaginative make-believe overlook social conditions. For example, stepmothers occur for real, and it is not helpful to them, or to their stepchildren, that their evil avatar haunts so many fairytale films as well as books, and has been established as a natural, and useful, device to help a child grow up.

With regard to the fathers, brothers, and lovers, Bettelheim shows a bias, born of his time and place, of which he seems to remain entirely unaware. Discussing the close of 'Little Red Cap', when the huntsman arrives in the nick of time and cuts the little girl and her grandmother out of the belly of the wolf, Bettelheim approves strongly of this ending: 'The male is . . . all-important, split into two opposite forms: the dangerous seducer who, if given in to, turns into the destroyer . . . and the hunter, the responsible strong, and rescuing father figure' (see Figures 8 and 13).

The Uses of Enchantment is long, rich, and detailed, and this summary does not do it justice. Besides, the book is so successful that its ideas have themselves become agents in forming the social context in which fairy tales now circulate, shaping the decisions of the entertainment industry and the publishers' markets, and establishing them as prime conduits of knowledge for the young, the adolescent, and their parents (Angela Carter pungently termed this approach 'house-training the Id'). Along with many readers and students, I learned a huge amount from Bettelheim, though he enrages me as he has done many other lovers of fairy tales—especially feminists who take issue with the psychoanalytic premises about female nature, destiny, and sexual identity. Carter defiantly closes her riposte, 'The Company of Wolves', to 'Red Riding Hood' with the little girl happily tucked up with the wolf: 'See! Sweet and sound she sleeps in granny's bed, between the paws of the tender wolf.' And the American artist Kiki Smith, in an enthralling and uncanny sculpture called *Daughter*, created a dreaming hairy-faced wolf child—the offspring of Red Riding Hood and the wolf.

The intertwining of psychoanalysis and fairy tale has been tight, and the stories are still trusted to offer a key to understanding the human psyche—regardless of history or social circumstances. Carl Jung, Freud's former cherished ally, broke away to found his own branch of analysis, which values fairy tales as the creations of humanity's collective unconscious. His theories about the archetypes encountered in the stories—the Maiden, the Crone, the Eternal Youth, and others—are gaining in popularity and have also profoundly shaped the trust in fairy tales as coded wisdom about how to grow up, how to pass safely through the stages of life, and the ordeals and choices the passage brings. The belief that the stories have the power to lead by example and shape character, especially gender, to engineer social citizens, and inculcate values and ideology has been widely held and is still accepted. Even if we are persuaded (as I am) that fairy tales are somehow 'real' documents of the past, we don't need to know anything about Black Forest husbandry or medieval marriage arrangements to recognize ourselves in the plots of 'Red Riding Hood', 'Sleeping Beauty', 'Hansel and Gretel', or 'The Boy Who Wanted to Learn How to Shudder'. The trials confronted in fairy tales reach deep into the psyche, even when starvation, forced marriage, or abandonment in a foundling hospital are no longer very likely (though I am aware that there are still many occurrences).

Making a Man of Him

Much of the critical thinking, from *The Uses of Enchantment* to the Jungian analyst Marie-Luise von Franz's ruminations, shows more interest in the female fairy tales than in the hero tales. All the favourite and famous fairy tales today are girls' stories—romances, rather than 'bloods' as adventure stories for boys were known in the booksellers' trade. But while the stories' views of femaleness and femininity have been thoroughly shaken up, assumptions about maleness and masculinity have not been interrogated as enterprisingly—there's been a reluctance to address the question, and a general retreat from even thinking about boys and fairy tales, probably because doing so leads into very deep waters about what society expects from young men—and these are proving hard to plumb.

'The Boy Who Wanted to Learn How to Shudder' tells a tale about the making of a man, and it gives an insight into the extent of the problem of maleness and masculinity in fairy tale. Its original title has been translated in many ways: the more common version, 'The boy who set out to learn fear', fails to catch the humour and the ordinary, embodied character of his eventual discovery, and, with that embodiment, the story's double entendre. It is a boys' initiation story, analogous to 'Red Riding Hood', but very different, as lads in fairy tales vividly capture gender opposition. Often a simpleton or Dummling, the hero outfoxes the cleverest adversary and surpasses the strongest; he wins wealth, power, and the princess regardless of merit or effort—many boys' fairy tales are compensatory fantasies.

'The Boy Who...' opens with a hero who's never afraid. He passes unscathed through a series of fearsome and ghoulish tests, and never shrinks: hanged men from a gallows, a haunted castle, a game of skittles with skulls and bones. Nothing daunts him. Until, that is, the princess he has won by his prowess tips a bucket of minnows over him in bed: 'The little fish wriggled all over him. He woke up with a start and shouted, "Oh, I've got the creeps. I've got the creeps, dear wife!"'

This is how the young man learns fear—in bed with his wife, not battling an ogre. This is downhome male banter (with a tinge of the dirty joke), and it shows that the meaning of a tale depends on the audience.

When the Third Reich identified the Grimms' stories as national heritage, this comic Gothic tale was taken as a kind of how-to guide to being hard; the Nazis embedded some of their favourites in the school curriculum and encouraged film interpretations. No less than twenty-three live action films were made, and included ghastly and dismaying scenes, including

Red Riding Hood rescued by an SS officer from an anti-Semitic cartoon wolf. During the process of de-Nazification, the Grimms were banned from schools and libraries; they had formed part of the propaganda machine for turning out fascists, and the Allies saw them as irredeemably tainted.

More than half the Grimms' tales star a young hero. He overcomes ogres, trounces stingy employers, and wins a haughty princess by daring, wit, and wiles (see Figure 11). But he's not a Terminator. Often there's no reason for his success—he begins, as in 'The Boy Who...', as a good-for-nothing lazybones. While the fairytale genre generally ignores patient merit, it does concern itself with the downtrodden and the ill used, and a central part of its consolations derives from fate's twists and turns. The odds are stacked against everyone, more or less equally, and everything can change, suddenly, without rhyme or reason. The impenetrability of destiny and the helplessness of humans in the grip of chance count among the sharpest messages of fairy tale, and the explanatory tools, psychoanalytical or other, blunt themselves on their mystery.

There are dozens of such Cinderella protagonists—youths as well as girls—and editors, publishers, and film-makers have generally preferred stories of heroic rescue and mayhem. But the Nazis dramatized them in earnest to a political purpose, whereas the Victorians and Edwardians tended to bluff, sometimes grotesque comedy, stressing the silly wishfulness of a story in which a tailor swats seven flies in a single blow.

The problem of the hero still stirs: in 1990, the poet Robert Bly took it up boldly and caused a furore with his book, *Iron*

John: A Book about Men, in which he argued a new approach to manliness. He chose one of the lesser-known Grimm tales, 'Iron Hans', or 'Iron John', about a mysterious encounter between a youth and a shaggy giant who lives in the depths of a forest pool where he keeps untold riches. Bly gave the fairy tale an allegorical reading that stresses the need for masculine virtues (bravery, forbearance, and comradeship) and proposed older mentors for youths. For a while, a men's movement flourished in the US, with Iron John as their role model. Since that attempt was widely mocked, others have stepped in: Arthur Frank, invoking men's alliances in myths and fairy tales, has developed an ideal of male companionship and bonding in mutual tenderness and support; similarly, a Jungian therapist, Craig Stephenson, in a fine study of madness, draws on alternative mythic and folk heroes, such as the spellbound, metamorphosing Sweeney, an alter ego of Seamus Heaney from the Celtic tradition. Both these writers are highly sensitized to the admiration and encouragement of violence in the public sphere and have been struggling—it is tempting to say, manfully—to foster friendlier and more interesting variants on masculinity than the usual princes, giant-killers, and ne'er-do-wells. *Reading Boyishly*, a highly original and courageous study by the art historian Carol Mavor, draws attention to the softness and vulnerability of the adolescent male; she even attempts to transvalue the much derided cissy. Looking through her eyes, fairy tales for boys, alongside a great many other cultural products, are indeed bent on disciplining them to be manly by being tough, just as ideologically as the girls' stories hold up a vision of female virtues.

The language of symbols is more mutable and arbitrary than common parlance, and words and terms are always shifting in meaning likewise. Although the premise for Freud's analysis is that the stories have universal meaning, most decodings remain subjective and, being subjective, are shaped by a mesh of circumstances (personal and social), contradictory and as numerous as their makers and inconsistent with one another. One way to answer the problem about boys and fairy tales is to look at the context in which a particular story was told—psychoanalysis itself forged its interpretive keys according to presumptions of gender and value, and they are now being recast in response to changing conditions. Another necessary line of enquiry looks at the history of selection. Any anthology will yield little-known tales which present a different picture of maleness, just as they will reveal plucky, witty, trickster heroines. But historically over a long period of cultural artefacts, gallant, loyal, and loving characters have been eclipsed.

Psychological readings are far more popular than any socio-historical analysis, and have excited a vast secondary literature of therapy, self-help and how-to books, the personal growth industry and academic literary criticism. Any one of us could mention titles—many of them huge bestsellers—that throw a psychoanalytic light on fairy tales—*Women Who Run with the Wolves*, by Clarissa Pinkola Estés, a wildfire bestseller after it came out in 1992, unfolds fairy tales as potent elixirs for female self-renewal.

The stories provoke and enrage, as well as inspire, enlighten, and entertain. It is really up to us—what stories we choose to tell, what we see in them, how we tell them. Not everyone is happy to agree with Red Riding Hood when she tells herself, 'You'll never stray from the path into the forest by yourself again, not ever for the rest of your life, when your mother has told you not to.'

Feminists were prominent among those who began talking back. They identified—and identify—strongly with the tradition, as its prime subject matter and as its voices. Aroused by Freud's question, 'What do women want?', which lies at the centre of conjectures made by (mostly male) analysts, they seized hold of fairy tales and shook them till the stories choked, spat out the poison, and sat up ready for a different day.

7

In the Dock

Don't Bet on the Prince

'Is it dark down there, Prince Horrendous?
Dark down there with Betsy Skull?
Is it dark down there
Where the grass grows through the hair?
Is it dark in the under-land of Null?'

Helen Adam, 'Down There in the Dark'

In the post-war period, women who had been brought up on fairy tales, and who had been taken to the Disney animation classics *Snow White* (1937) and *Cinderella* (1950), rose up and protested against the lies and stereotyping in the stories, the wishful thinking, the distorted values, the beauty queen fantasies, and the pervasive bad faith of the promise, 'and they lived happily ever after'. They further attacked the way re-tellers and films sanitized the original stories, taming them in order to indoctrinate small children and adolescents even more deceitfully. Fairy tales were denounced as a blunt tool of patriarchy, the bourgeoisie, cosmetic surgeons, the fashion industry, and psychoanalysts bent on curbing girls' energies and desires.

In Basile's fairy tale, 'Sole, Luna, e Talia' (Sun, Moon, and Thalia), the heroine is a Sleeping Beauty (Figure 13), and is raped while she lies unconscious—but Perrault draws a veil over this side of things.

A favourite heroine, such as the Grimm Brothers' Little Red Cap, fails to use her wits and escape from the wolf, whereas the spirited, but much less well-known Dalila the Wily from the *Nights* runs rings around her adversaries, and the beloved of the Ram, in D'Aulnoy's tale, rejects him till he expires of grief. By contrast, the deep malice of the witches and evil stepmothers, the unrelieved spite of some sisters, and the murderous jealousy between mothers and daughters were left to stand, unchallenged. These portraits of female evil supported male interests, too. The tales were not merely symptoms but also instruments of a strategy: divide women against one another the better to lord it over them. Furthermore, in a more settled and prosperous world, the longing in fairy tales for a safer, more comfortable life looked like rank consumerism and cynical upward mobility, cost what may. Such materialistic values stuck in the craw of women determined to build a world in which marriage was not a business transaction, and their inner well-being and nourishment mattered. Subversion became the battle cry: the tales were to be turned inside out and upside down.

The first step was critical reading, to expose how the tales are not primordial, intact vessels of peasant wisdom, but expressions of the collectors' and authors' values, which are both time-bound and class-bound. The scholar Ruth Bottigheimer,

Figure 13 'She was so lovely she seemed, almost, to shine...'. 'Sleeping Beauty', from *Household Stories from the Collection of the Brothers Grimm*, illustrated by Walter Crane, 1893.

in her book *Grimms' Bad Girls and Bold Boys* (1989), demonstrated how Wilhelm Grimm's endless tinkering tended to excuse the men and blame the women, whittling down heroines' words and granting boys more and more to do and to say. For example, besides introducing a father figure to save Little Red Cap, he progressively altered 'Hansel and Gretel' to explain away the father's conduct altogether. In the 1812 version, both the natural mother and father agree to abandon the children; by 1857 and the final edition, the father pleads with the woman, who has become a stepmother, and she overrules him. In the most notorious example of Wilhelm's interference, he censored the story of Rapunzel. In the first version, Rapunzel lets down her hair for the witch, and when she has climbed up into the tower as usual, Rapunzel asks her why her clothes are getting so tight. The witch realizes that in spite of keeping Rapunzel locked up and out of sight of man or beast, the young girl has been seeing someone . . . so she cuts off her hair and throws her out, to have her babies—for she is having twins—alone in the wilderness.

Through all the fantastic and extreme details, the truth-telling of this story, about teenage pregnancy, is plain—and eloquent.

But the frankness was too much for Wilhelm, and he changed Rapunzel's question to 'Tell me, Dame Godmother, how is it that you are much heavier to draw up than the young king's son, who only takes a moment to reach me?'

The scene turns Rapunzel into a ninny, whereas before she was clearly a victim of ignorance, and the tale an unapologetic call for sex education for the young.

Wilhelm's prudishness contrasts his toughness, however, when it came to savage and cruel actions: he could argue that it was a good thing to tell a dreadful story about murder in order to warn children about the consequences of their actions, but he withdrew from communicating the facts of life to little girls and boys through fairy tale. Yet this function must be one of the most deep-rooted of all.

Feminists grasped this role of the fairy tale: sexual education in the broadest sense became the aim of their subversions.

Awakenings

The Madwoman in the Attic, by the American literary scholars Sandra Gilbert and Susan Gubar, was a path-breaking study of Victorian women's writing, and it came out in 1979, four years after Bettelheim's *Uses of Enchantment*. Gilbert and Gubar put feminist readings centre stage as the supreme lens for understanding women's situation. They did not oppose Bettelheim altogether, but built on his insights. The evil stepmother in 'Snow White' inspired them to a blazing assault on the presuppositions Bettelheim shared with the Grimms, and a defence of the active, mobile, powerful older woman, so often vilified in the stories.

After critical close readings of fairy tales, the strategies feminists devised ranged from furious satire, irony, and parody and, at the other end of the literary spectrum, romancing on their own terms, in inventive and witty re-visionings—to use the term of the poet Adrienne Rich. Re-visioning the tales as scriptures for the women's revolution involved combining and recombining the elements to galvanize them into new life.

BOX 5   *The Anger of Anne Sexton*

The American poet Anne Sexton blazes with scorn of fairytale promises in her 1971 volume *Transformations*. In a series of scalding twists on the best-loved heroine tales, delivered in a vivid mixture of slang and poetic metaphor, she invokes a Cinderella turned Stepford wife, condemned to a life of utter banality:

> Cinderella and the prince
> lived, they say, happily ever after,
> like two dolls in a museum case
> never bothered by diapers or dust,
> never arguing over the timing of an egg,
> never telling the same story twice,
> never getting a middle-aged spread,
> their darling smiles pasted on for eternity.
> Regular Bobbsey Twins.
> That story.

With her version of Briar Rose (Sleeping Beauty) she touches darker depths:

> Little doll child,
> come here to Papa.
> Sit on my knee.
> I have kisses for the back of your neck.
> A penny for your thoughts, Princess.
> I will hunt them like an emerald.

The response then insinuatingly indicts this fatherly voice from an omniscient angle, coincidental with ours, the readers', looking on:

> It's not the prince at all,
> but my father
> drunkeningly bends over my bed,

> circling the abyss like a shark,
> my father thick upon me
> like some sleeping jellyfish.

Beneath Anne Sexton's nightmarish vision, you can glimpse the broken trust in families, as well as the suffocating limits on women's horizons. You can hear the desperation that drove women mad.

Sexton was in treatment for mental distress most of her life, including long psychoanalysis, and her savaging fairy tales expresses her frustration against her state. But rethinking fairy tales didn't manage to lift Sexton's own darkness, and in 1974, three years after *Transformations* came out, she committed suicide.

These retellings often take the form of what have been called 'anti-tales': they seize hold of the old story and 'tell it slant'. Yet the magnetic pull of fairy tales, especially on women, could not be resisted, it seems, and the work of subversion gave them added power over the female imagination. Jack Zipes is one of the male writers who joined in the campaign of ideological exposure, with a pioneer study called *Breaking the Magic Spell* (1979)—a sustained Marxist-inflected invective against commodification and Disneyfication (quasi-synonymous). Beneath Zipes's tirades, there burns the anger of a lover betrayed, for he is a passionate champion of fairy tales and continued advocate for their intrinsic, emancipatory value. He follows Walter Benjamin, who proclaimed, in 'The Storyteller' essay, that the fairy tale has power to set minds free: '[The storyteller] has counsel, not for a few situations, as the proverb does, but for many, like the sage. The storyteller is the figure in which the right-eous man encounters himself.'

What does this belief mean? How does it materialize in fairy tales, especially regarding women? The most incandescent work to rise from the feminist explosion is undoubtedly *The Bloody Chamber* by Angela Carter, a stretch of virtuoso imaginative writing and a potent critique. The ten fairy tales—a kind of profane Decalogue—came out the same year as *The Madwoman in the Attic*, 1979, and have been gaining more and more readers year on year, inspiring young women now who could be Carter's grandchildren.

Carter wanted to open up the tales, she said, to reveal their latent, erotic content. In consummately stylish, baroque prose poetry, she picks up stock figures, bright images, plot reversals, and condenses them with hallucinatory intensity. In the title story, Carter seems to have opened the forbidden door for a generation of young women with her vision of Bluebeard as a languid connoisseur of every depravity, half beast, half *ancien régime* tyrant, who unexpectedly arouses her: 'For the first time in my innocent and confined life, I sensed in myself a potentiality for corruption that took my breath away.'

In 'The Erl-King', a title which evokes Goethe's spooky ballad about Death chasing a child, Carter remembers Schubert's setting, but she folds into the tale Orphic memories, bird metamorphoses (from the Grimms' 'Jorinda and Joringel'), murderer bridegrooms, and a trickster heroine who defeats her abductor—all in seven pages. 'The Snow Child' is her version of 'Snow White'; it does not reject the fairy tale's vision of vicious internecine jealousy between women, but instead pushes it to extremes until the reader

can't but notice the horror of the power relations evoked—
and thereby, perhaps, learn to resist them.

Carter is a knowing old she-wolf leading cubs, like her
own feral 'Wolf Alice', into the dark and fascinating wind-
ings of sexual desire. But her gleeful mischief-making, often
in these murkier corners of sexuality, caused many of her
sisters in the movement to reject Carter, and she remains a
controversial and maverick figure. This is as she would have
wished. As she also said, 'a tale...retains a singular moral
function—that of provoking unease.'

The Bloody Chamber has become the founding charter of
modern fairy tale, and the catalyst of a million awakenings
for readers (especially girls) coming upon it for the first time.
It is not too much to claim that Carter's writing also changed
the landscape of the genre. Certainly, in my own case
(and I think I am typical), it gave me new, vital carnal
knowledge. However, unlike most fairy tales, and certainly
unlike the majority of the erotic fantasies selling fast today,
her writing dazzles: her prose is unabashed in its festivity,
lacerating scorn, and salty pungency. She puts on a performance of brilliant kinetic energy, displaying masterly
handling of register, irony, allusion, phrase, and lexicon.
She is playful, richly layered, and exuberantly fearless as
she attempts to reconfigure new possible worlds—where
the heroines will not submit but will understand their
own appetites and act to fulfil them, where social structures
will not constrict free spirits. The contents have been
much imitated; the imagery of bondage and prohibited
female sensuality has given many lesser talents permission
to write Mummy Porn, but none of these resonances

are the responsibility of Carter herself or of fairy tales themselves.

You could say that the fairy tale grew up in 1979. That same year, Angela Carter issued a deliberate and outrageous provocation, an essay called *The Sadeian Woman*; in it, she upheld the pornography of the Marquis de Sade as a feminist tool of illumination. It was published by the new feminist house, Virago Press. What Carter had found in fairy tales of Perrault, Grimm, and (later) D'Aulnoy were profoundly disturbing symptoms of men's assumed hegemony and women's collusion with their oppression and sexual exploitation; yet she loved the stories and spent time translating them as well as responding to them.

Later in her writing career, Angela Carter became a collector of stories. She didn't re-vision the tales or indeed edit or retouch them. Instead, she collected from all over the world. The resulting two volumes radiate a far jollier spirit of resistance than *The Bloody Chamber*. She mustered a gaggle of unruly, bold, clever, trickster girls (not a Snow White victim among them) as well as a band of incorrigible powerful older women: she loved a beldame. She brought them in from the corners of folklore's cobwebbed attics, dusted them down, and arranged them in sections called 'Good Girls and Where It Gets Them', 'Strong Minds and Low Cunning', and 'Beautiful People'. As a woman and a writer, she wants to have it both ways: the tale shadowed by the anti-tale, the hope trailing a weight of irony.

That period of excitement and protest still carries a powerful charge: Angela Carter's name, more than twenty years after her death, can still fill a hall like a rock star. But she was herself very sceptical about the difference she or anyone else could make, and acutely aware of the warnings sounded by philosophers, such as Herbert Marcuse and Theodor Adorno, that under the present arrangements of markets and media there can be no subversive act or work that will not end up absorbed, and de-fanged. Yet she did not give up the struggle. Just as love of fairy tales drew her to them irresistibly while loathing of their values roused her to disfigure their sweetness, so romance and cynicism are entangled in her ferocious refashionings. She was a utopian and a satirist, and a fight between idealism and despair flourished, unresolved, inside her.

The contrary spirit of the feminist fairy tale has also enlivened the growth of Young Adult fiction, with unflinching fantasists exploring the lives of girls—and some boys—through revisiting 'Rapunzel', 'Snow White', and other classics. The furious feminist protests of the Seventies have become axioms of children's publishing and of film producers' brainstorming sessions. Hungry film companies in the vast global entertainment industry commission women screenwriters like Linda Woolverton, who has written the scripts for Disney's *Mulan*, about the Chinese warrior princess, *Beauty and the Beast*, and *Aladdin*. Featuring upbeat, spirited, and physically vigorous heroines, such films are clearly answering the demand for positive role models. Often they show the strain, however, producing ideology even as they bend backwards to avoid it, for example in *Tangled*, in which the heavily ironic opening song, 'Mother knows best', continues unequivocally to uphold teenage rebellion and cast blame on older female authority figures. But overall, the critiques of both psychoanalysts and feminists, as they probed the dark secret loves at the sick heart of fairy tale, have transfigured the genre.

Patriarchal Attitudes by Eva Figes was in the vanguard of the post-war feminism when it was published in 1970; a whole generation later, Figes wrote *Tales of Innocence and Experience* (2003) a compelling and tender account of her relationship with a granddaughter. They read fairy tales together, and Figes observes the complexity of the little girl's responses and shades these loving, perceptive observations with another story, about her own childhood long ago, and then, less personally, about the dilemmas that fairy tales still set women. The author's memories of Berlin before the war, of her family's persecution as Jews, of her father's imprisonment and lucky—extremely lucky—reprieve, and their departure for exile in London in 1939, ebb and flow through her mind as she watches over and cares for her granddaughter. Her own grandparents died in the camps: this knowledge alters, deeply alters the impact of the fate of the granny in 'Red Riding Hood'. She does not tell her grandchild this story.

Every story can be retold differently: Eva Figes is rawly aware, throughout, of the effect of fairy tales, as Lang was when he selected and edited and recast the material, as Carter was when she so gleefully exposed it. Figes pictures the enraptured attention she can command as she reads, and the emotions—the anxiety, the identification, and the sympathy—which flare up and then die down again: the scenes of reading and telling here can lead to consolation, to gratified desire. Yet throughout, Eva Figes is alive to the perils on the way:

> It is part of the story-time ritual that I put my right arm round her, giving comfort and security, whilst I turn the pages with my left hand. Daylight beyond the window, slanting across the page. I stop to point out incidental details in the coloured illustration, an owl perched on a branch, the roof of the ginger-bread house, which looks deliciously edible. I reiterate, as I have done on previous occasions, that witches do not exist in real life, only in stories.

The deaths of mothers, the wickedness of stepmothers, the appetite of ogres, the complicity of their brides, the parents who abandon their children: all these harsh features of fairy tales throw up one storytelling challenge after another. Figes pauses on 'Snow White':

> I continue with the sad tale of Snow-White, conceived in midwinter, with her black hair and her unearthly skin, her mother duly dying as the child was born.
>
> Alarm bells ring in my head even as I read out the words. Hastily I explain that in the olden days, long, long ago, women did occasionally die when they had a baby, but not now, definitely not. My daughter is expecting her second child, and her first-born is beginning to show quite sufficient signs of childish insecurity as it is, without worrying about losing her mother entirely . . .

The bedtime ritual, as the child nestles with her granny, mitigates—melts—the iciness of the threat in the tale; but it might also not be sufficient, not provide enough warmth. As Figes remarks, 'Fright is fun, but only up to a point. Where the point is: that is the mystery.'

The brave assault which feminist writers led against fairy tales did indeed lay bare the latent contents, but with unforeseen consequences. The problems of female heroism are open to all questers, male and female, but they are now equipped with different knowledge and expectations than before, when they set out to cut a new trail through the rose briars.

8

Double Vision

The Dream of Reason

> ...the most private and ignorant wishful thinking is
> to be preferred to any mindless goose-stepping; for
> wishful thinking is capable of revolutionary aware-
> ness, and can enter the chariot of history without
> necessarily abandoning in the process the good con-
> tent of dreams.
>
> Ernst Bloch

The tradition of fairy tale has lent itself to some of the most acute intellectual creations in the name and interest of rationality. Writers have wrapped themselves in fairytale themes and motifs in order to communicate political and philosophical thinking, sometimes in conditions of censorship, sometimes in the interests of amusing their audience and so persuading them more effectively. This seems a paradox, but it is the case that satire, comedy, polemic, and sexual critique have adopted features of the genre as a cloak for their deeper intent; a literature of enchantment has flourished since the eighteenth century alongside mimetic and realist modes, as a distinctive but no less lucid mirror of mores and manners.

The generic characteristics of fairy tale are not introduced in earnest but in a spirit of play and parody. A plethora of stories knowingly mocks the conventions of the genre; with sly tongue-in-cheek, writers have adopted the form even while they are communicating a story with an urgent message. Occupying this playful double register, the fairy tale invites adults to experience it knowingly, their responses lying athwart the pleasure a child takes in the same material. The effect is to draw the carpet away from under the fantasy so that it remains enjoyable, but stops being believable. By this unexpectedly frequent manoeuvre, fairy tale becomes a prime vehicle of reason, as Angela Carter declares in the visionary concluding sentence of *The Bloody Chamber*. Wolf Alice is grooming the rank beast, licking the filth off him like a cat:

> The lucidity of the moonlight lit the mirror propped against the red wall; the rational glass, the master of the visible, impartially recorded the crooning girl.

Like a vampire, the Duke has no reflection. But, according to the active and punning metaphors of fairy tale, both girl and monster will become capable of reflection when they finally become visible to each other:

> As she continued her ministrations, this glass, with infinite slowness, yielded to the reflexive strength of its own material construction. Little by little, there appeared within it, like the image on photographic paper that emerges, first, a formless web of tracery, the prey caught in its own fishing net, then in

147

firmer yet still shadowed outline until at last as vivid as real life itself, as if brought into being by her soft, moist, gentle tongue, finally, the face of the Duke.

The beast bridegroom materializes under the motions of the heroine's tongue, which is the writer's tongue too, her language, which makes visible what fantasy invents. The fairy tale acts as a rational glass, and its impartial reflection ('as vivid as real life itself') brings the secondary world back to earth, beaming epiphanies about our own possible state of existence.

In the Know: Anti-tales and Parody

It would be easy to imagine that the parodic games of rational fabulists have arisen over time, as a result of familiarity with original fairytale material, and that they mark out contemporary rational scepticism and knowingness, even cynicism or misanthropy. Modern re-visionings certainly assume knowledge of the sources, as Carter does, and rekindle the old stories' fires. In this sense the modern or contemporary avatars of the genre are meta-fictions, and often absorbed into definitions of the postmodern. They quote, they parody, they pastiche, they masquerade in enchanted guises: the heroine Villanelle in Winterson's *The Passion* has webbed toes and walks on water; an ugly sister becomes a heroine in A.S. Byatt's 'The Eldest Princess' (1998); and in *Snow, Glass, Apples*, a ferociously cruel tale by Neil Gaiman, the wicked queen is sucked dry by the vampire child Snow White. But to see this as a modern form of metamorphosis is mistaken. The further back one goes, self-mockery and fairy tale have been deeply interwoven.

Apuleius undercuts his own romancing in 'Cupid and Psyche', first by giving the story to a disreputable old bawd to tell the poor abducted bride 'to make her feel a little better', and then by dramatizing her ghastly death at the hands of the bandits in contradiction of the tale's consoling promises: the framing turns his beautiful allegory of love into a mocking illusion. One of Apuleius's sources for *The Golden Ass* was a ribald fable, *The Ass*, by his Greek predecessor Lucius of Samosata. Lucius is the author of the brilliant short meta-fiction *The True History*, a fiercely comic and inventive story that probes, with unsurpassed acuity, the fictive nature of literature—and this, in the second century BC. Shakespeare, responding to Apuleius, grasps this duplicity of fairy vision (in *A Midsummer Night's Dream*) when Titania and the lovers become rapt in dreams but then wake to see reason. He gives us in the theatre the delight of entering enchantment and the comfort of returning to the reasonable ground of disenchantment—but not altogether. Shakespeare issues a manifesto for fairy tale's illusion when his Hippolyta rises to the defence of fancy:

> For all the story of the night told o'er,
> And all their minds transfigured altogether
> More witnesseth than fancy's images
> And grows to something of great constancy.

(*A Midsummer Night's Dream*, V.i.23–6)

Tzvetan Todorov has memorably divided fantasy into three kinds: supernatural, which offers divine intervention as explanation of wonders (myth, generally speaking); scientific, which posits astonishing and unexplained events and then uses them to illuminate and rationalize their mystery (sci-fi, as in Jules Verne, H. G. Wells, and Ursula Le Guin) and fantasy, his third and most resonant expression, which Todorov defines as a debatable land, a form of the Freudian Uncanny. Uncanny fantasy is enigmatic; it leaves the causes unexplained and the reader in doubt (Henry James's *The Turn of the Screw* is a tour de force in this mode). In their modern transformations, fairy tales can be sited in this version of the Uncanny, which then opens on to the possibilities of full-blown magical realism. But this is not the complete story, and the Todorovian categories fail to take account of the way fairy tale is poised, not between knowing and not knowing the causes of the wonders and enchantments, but between accepting them (as the ideal child reader does) and rejecting them (as the adult reader can be expected to do). The form however draws the latter into the stance of the former: we are not always placed in doubt as to what to believe, but rather invited to return to an imaginary state of trusting fictions, and this carries a special pleasure. The duality lies partly in the tale itself, but chiefly in ourselves as readers.

Chris Warnes, in his fine study *Magical Realism and the Postcolonial Novel* (2009), focuses instead on the polarity between faith and irreverence. He argues that writers of fantastic tales such as Miguel Angel Asturias, Gabriel García Márquez, and Isabel Allende draw on a body of vital indigenous folk beliefs, and appeal to a national community, identified with a particular mythical past in Latin America. He contrasts this use of enchantments very convincingly with the rational, demythologizing approach of other magical realists such as Robert Coover, Salman Rushdie,

Angela Carter, and Ali Smith, who disenchant the belief systems they draw on with multiple instruments of irony, satire, and burlesque. The Latin Americans, broadly speaking, do not undermine the structure of magic they create, whereas the North Americans and Europeans make a show of their scepticism (superiority to the very conventions they are using).

All magical realist fiction, whether believing or doubting, dips into the streams of fairy story for its material: Rushdie's sparkling children's novel, *Haroun and the Sea of Stories* (1990), takes up his predicament as an author under threat of censorship and death, and turns it into a classic quest adventure from the *Arabian Nights*: his child protagonist Haroun sets out on a chivalrous errand to save the wellsprings of story from pollution. And if magical realism is understood as a mode, rather than a time-bound development of the novel, then authors such as Swift, Voltaire, and Kafka have also found inspiration for their fantastic fiction in fairytale conventions: other worlds, talking animals, monsters, bodily transformations, improbable and hyperbolic plot developments, the stark opposition of good and evil. Voltaire wrote *contes philosophiques* (philosophical tales) as spoofs of Oriental narrative. Yet he had an appetite for marvels and drew on the literature of wonder, from fairy lore to travellers' tales for his lacerating attacks on contemporary mores and malpractices: his villains (Jesuits, for example) strike echoes with evil sorcerers, his despots and oppressors with ogres. In other words, the irrational tenets of religion and the fanciful products of the imagination, which Voltaire derided when they required blind belief, served him perfectly to channel his iconoclastic philosophy.

151

The folklore of central Europe and the Near East, Judaic and other, also provided Kafka with much raw material, and he deepens the enigmatic messages of his fables by twisting fairytale promises: the end of his most famous short tale, 'Metamorphosis', lifts towards hope as in a happy ending, but at the expense of Gregor Samsa, who has been swept away, a dead insect, by the maid. As Kafka said, 'There is hope, but not for us.' His inexhaustible fable gains power from interacting with fairytale norms, and then breaking them. In this case, most resonantly, no supernatural, scientific, or psychological cause is offered for Gregor's change; we are left in the dark. The effect is not however uncanny, but treated pragmatically as a simple fact, against all probability. Kafka learned matter-of-fact brevity from proverbial wisdom, Central European melancholy humour, and the harsh, laconic style of the Brothers Grimm, and his tales reverberate with a similar dark, wry fatalism, as for example in 'A Little Fable' (the cat eats the mouse), or 'The Song of the Sirens' (there is none), or in the savage tale 'Jackals and Arabs', which announces endless civil conflict in the desert. It is an animal parable, with animal anti-heroes who interact with humans and their folly. The closing lines, again in full consciousness of breaking faith with the reader, default on a promise of reprieve:

> 'You are right, sir,' said he, 'we'll leave them to their business; besides, it's time to break camp. Well, you've seen them. Marvellous creatures, aren't they? And how they hate us!'

Kafka allows no pay off; we are caught in the noose of the tale and its scenes of hatred and carnage forever. He takes fabulism far beyond the enchanted wood, into metaphysics and existential parable: Walter Benjamin commented that Kafka wrote 'fairy tales for dialecticians'.

Another admirer of Kafka, Jorge Luis Borges, in the short essay 'Kafka and his Precursors', argues that once Kafka had appeared, an entire, previously undiscovered continent of literature rose, a kind of Atlantis on the horizon behind him; similarly, Kafka himself in turn crystallizes an approach to legends, parables, and the wonder tale that has shaped an entire succession of writers, who continue to create dialectical fairy tales.

In conditions of censorship, for example, writers have resorted to folk narrative as protective camouflage: fairy tales open a door to political fable, the tyrants and ogres *could* be cast down, justice restored and equality achieved. Avant-garde writers, such as the artist Kurt Schwitters in Germany, Béla Balázs in Hungary, and Karel Čapek in Prague, composed many high-spirited, absurdist, and heartfelt utopian fairy stories, intended to mould the soft wax of young citizens towards dreams of a new human nature—or to attack the status quo. It was Karel and his brother Josef who in 1922 coined the word 'robot', in their blackly comic satire about the fate of workers in factories, *RUR or Rossum's Universal Robots*. During the worst days of repression, when the early socialist hopes lay in ruins, rebels still found a means of expression in fantastic tales; and these could sometimes manage to elude the censors' scissors.

Impossible Dreamers: Keeping Out of Hell

The fairy tales scholar Jessica Tiffin observes perceptively that fairy tale as a genre carries within it a contradiction between conformity and revolt: 'The ideological implications of this continuing popularity [in the mass media] are complex and at times problematical, given fairy tale's peculiarly coherent surface and its ability to give a deeply satisfying and utopian gloss to assumptions about society, power, and gender which are often profoundly reactionary.' The conservatism of the form makes its appeal, especially to dissidents, even more noteworthy. Yet the two greatest contemporary masters of the rational mode of fairy tale, Italo Calvino and Angela Carter, were both self-declared leftists, and Carter, younger than Calvino, was deeply shaped by his imaginative solutions.

Calvino's parents were both biologists (he first enrolled as a student in the sciences), and he brought scientific method to literature with marvellous flair. His exhaustive trawl through Italian fairy tales changed him as a writer and he turned away from the quasi-cinematic Neo-Realism of his early fiction to devise strange literary taxonomies—in novels that are brilliantly agile variations on Propp's anatomy of folk tales. For Calvino, who, like his parents, was an anti-Fascist (he fought as a partisan), agnostic, and anti-clerical, fairy tale was ultimately more honest about literature than realism—*verismo*—because it admitted its own condition as illusion. This made it a mode of choice for someone who was searching for an ethics for society and individuals, and wanted to avoid fraudulent storytelling.

A literature that does not make false claims about its truthfulness, but owns up to its fictive condition, fitted his idealism more surely than literary attempts at faithful imitation of life. And Calvino has a fecund, indeed inexhaustible, imagination for active metaphor and fully formed allegory, at times couched in scientific language (*Cosmicomics*, 1969), at times in topographical flights as breathtaking as any story from the *Nights*, thronged with wonders. His most beautiful novel, *Invisible Cities* (1972), conjures fifty-five castles in the air, as it were, and then meditates, in lapidary, exquisite dialogues between Marco Polo and 'the Great Khan', on the varieties of their peoples and customs. Its closing lines crystallize his sensitivity to fairy tale's false promises, when Polo says, 'There are two ways to escape suffering it [inferno]. The first is easy for many: accept the inferno and become such a part of it that you can no longer see it. The second is risky and demands constant vigilance and apprehension: seek and learn to recognize who and what, in the midst of inferno, are not inferno, then make them endure, give them space.'

These words have been justly quoted again and again: they communicate Calvino's philosophy, his wise storyteller's counsel, as well as a description of the best function of fable and fairy tale.

Like her Italian contemporary, Angela Carter read widely and deeply in fairy tale; she worked on the corpus in a historical and scholarly fashion, was steeped in the slippery ironies of D'Aulnoy and Perrault. In her hands, fairy tale is always written in a double register, with serious romances ('The Lady in the House of Love' and 'Puss-in-Boots')

155

striking notes of rude bawdy, and her deep love of the genre undercut by her feline, even arch knowingness. These overtones serve her political intentions: to expose the prerogatives of aristocrats, fathers, and other authorities, to liberate the libido of young women from the taboos of *politesse*, to tell things how they are—and how they could be. In these respects, Carter is a true daughter of Voltaire and of Kafka, an advocate of Enlightenment, who forged fairy tales into instruments of rational enquiry and scriptures for emancipation. In a firework display of radio plays, film scripts, and novels (as well as the short fictions) she continued her assault on the genre in a spirit of fiery love—and hate. In *Nights at the Circus* (1984), the title gestures to the *Arabian Nights*, while Fevvers, the colossal trapeze artist heroine, spreads her purple dyed wings, and flies. 'Is she fact or is she fiction?' keeps recurring as a question in the novel. Again, in the interests of truth-telling, a fairytale impossibility—a winged woman—allows the author to call attention to herself as an honest broker.

Nights at the Circus was followed by another ambitious novel, *Wise Children*, which was to be Carter's last book. An affectionate concoction, brewed from Shakespeare's comic romances, this novel also performs a series of extreme, ebullient variations on a vast set of traditional motifs (foundlings, twins, rags-to-riches trajectories, and back again).

Rational dreamers are still reflecting on gender, on effects of the new media, concepts of the self, relations of human beings with the natural world, and ways of avoiding hell. Some engagement with political visions continues in the fairytale tradition, both in the wake of the mordant modernists, and of their utopian predecessors (Dickens staging phantoms to torment Scrooge, and George MacDonald disguising gentle and eccentric sermons as whimsical fairy tales). Philip Pullman's heroine, Lyra, is given a truth-telling device, an 'alethiometer'. Like George MacDonald's Golden Key, it's a magical instrument that will lead to better worlds and better understanding. The traumatic scene of animal metamorphosis returns in Marie Darieussecq's 1996 best-seller, *Truismes* (Pig Tales) a fierce, Voltairean satire of lust and greed; the acerbic essayist and novelist Dubravka Ugrešić mischievously unleashes three hags for our time in *Baba Yaga Laid an Egg*; while the film *Spirited Away* (2001), by the Japanese master animator Hayao Miyazaki, issues a Swiftian manifesto against consumerism.

The fairytale repertory of fantastic possibilities continues to provide writers and others with a fine scalpel to probe and test the conditions of daily survival, and then imagine alternatives and redress.

9

On Stage & Screen

States of Illusion

Now I always knew
Fairy tales could come true
Today's hard fact was once a fairy tale.

Velimir Khlebnikov

Like many little girls, Princess Victoria was ballet-struck, and her most favourite prima ballerina of all—worth five enraptured exclamation marks and quadruple underscoring in her journals—was Marie Taglioni, who was the first to pad her dancing slippers so that she could lift up on her tiptoes and intensify the impression of ethereal lightness that was so desired by the Romantic choreographers of the classical ballet. The future Queen filled pages of her watercolour albums with paintings of the fairy vision of Taglioni *en pointe* and the corps de ballet of swans or wilis or sylphides fluttering in their frothy tutus and gauzy wings. These are the only direct allusions to fairy tale in her journals, and in this Victoria represents a widespread phenomenon, often overlooked in discussion of fairy tale and attempts to define the form. Fairy tales have never been exclusively verbal, and the slippery interactions of oral and written transmission over the course of the genre's history result as much from the stories' constant reincarnations on stage and on screen, from pantomime to puppet shows, again showing its affinity with migrating tunes, cross-pollinating plants. C. S. Lewis pointed out that fairy tales don't have to be great works of fiction, or even especially well written, to be unforgettable. Elite children like Princess Victoria emerged in the nineteenth and early twentieth centuries as the prime audience for *The Nutcracker* ballet or the opera of *Hansel and Gretel*, but the current is running firmly now towards larger and larger audiences, all over the world, and darker and more disturbing treatments, in the theatre, the cinema, and on television.

'What a joy it is to dance and sing!'

The libretti of ballets such as *The Sleeping Beauty*, *Swan Lake*, and many others invent this and borrow that, crystallizing various elements from national folklore (Russian folk tales) and literary classics (Perrault, E. T. A. Hoffmann). The raw materials are not, however, always readily identifiable, but have been transformed freely by the creators' imagination: *The Firebird* and *Giselle* are original dramatic works in their own right. Yet they are also essentially fairy tales, composed by bricolage with features that define the genre: supernatural and mysterious beings, a prevailing atmosphere of enchantment and vulnerability to destiny, and opening onto another, imaginary world that is only accessible through the work of art. And they are also, by definition, performed; their effect produced by a combination of skills carried out by a group, the ultimate origin or responsibility for the work distributed across a number of participants. Both as an arte-fact and as a process, a fairytale ballet, play, opera, or film reveals the reason that the genre is hard to pin down: it is a narrative, the labour of many hands in constant action over time, not tied to a specific medium, and its manifestations are fluid; they do not keep still.

When sung, stories also shape-shift into new, unprece-dented forms, and composers of opera have mined classic tales and national folklore for material: *Der Freischutz* (The Freeshooter, 1811) by Carl Maria von Weber is the source for the proverbial phrase 'silver bullet' after the magic instru-ment given to the hero in this opera's libretto; Jaroslav Kvapil, for the libretto of Dvořák's tragic and beautiful opera *Rusalka*, drew on a Czech Undine tale; in *Bluebeard's Castle* Bartók and Balázs profoundly reinterpret Perrault to create a metaphysical drama. Far lesser known fairy tales, written by the Venetian wit, playwright, and defender of traditional theatre Carlo Gozzi (1720–1806), have inspired composers, from Wagner's first opera, *Die Feen* (The Fairies), to Hans Werner Henze's fabulous epic *L'Upupa* (The Hoo-poe), a reworking of the *Nights*.

The case of Gozzi, the last, self-declared, and valiant cham-pion of the old *commedia dell'arte* conventions, discloses the connection that binds modern fairy tale to theatre. In a spirit of enlightened, light-footed scepticism, Gozzi concocted joyful fantasies from his wanderings through the

Arabian Nights, Basile's *Pentamerone*, and other collections of fairy tales. Interestingly, it was the *féeries* or court entertainments of the seventeenth century, counterparts of the *commedia*, that established the rich colloquy between flights of fancy and fairy illusions on stage. Renaissance court masques and the later *féeries* in royal palaces and in noblemen and noblewomen's chateaux mustered Italian players in extravagant décors and arrayed them in exotic costumes to mount spectacular events. Dance, music, slapstick, celebration, ritual, and pageantry coalesced in these mythological performances. *Féeries* were also the chief spur to the spectacular inventions of stage machines: flying chariots, underwater voyages, seven-league boots, devils exploding with fireworks, and other marvellous, extremely ambitious effects of great ingenuity.

The running interactions between fairy tale and performed media continue more vigorously than ever today, but the example of Gozzi also illuminates a crucial dimension of modern fairy tale: its emergence in symbiosis with the Enlightenment.

The plots, characterization, and libretti of ballets and operas have been thought of all too readily as mere pretexts for display or coathangers for the gorgeous raiment of music. Fortunately, the experience of going to a production of *La Cenerentola*, *Die Frau ohne Schatten* (Hofmannsthal's original libretto for Richard Strauss), *Blond Eckbert* (Judith Weir, based on a tale by Ludwig Tieck) reveals how mistaken and how limiting this view is, and, by and large, it has been superseded. Today, when a composer and librettist open horizons on to the marvellous they plunge deep into the streams of story in order to attain a more intense

161

Figure 14 Unlikely divas: three sisters are turned into singing fruit. *The Love for Three Oranges*, opera by Serge Prokofiev (1921), at the Paris Opera, directed by Gilbert Deflo, 2005.

enveloping experience—often the *Gesamtkunstwerk* that Wagner proclaimed. Prokofiev's opera, *The Love for Three Oranges* (Figure 14), draws inspiration from a very weird and wonderful tale by Gozzi, who took it from Basile in his most madcap mood.

But the intertwining of opera and ballet with enchantment does not entail that we who are listening submit to any particular cosmology invoked by the story—the *deus* or *dea ex machina* is not brought before us to invite our belief in their existence beyond the stage. We are not asked to clap our hands to say we believe in fairies (except by Barrie). Nor do we have to suspend our disbelief; the fairies, sorceresses, mermaids, and sprites excite a different kind of consent and one that is bound up with the period when dance and opera emerged in the multimedia entertainments we experience today. Opera is not sacred oratorio sung in church, nor is it a reprise of bacchanalian ritual. It absorbs their function, but as an art form, it came into being in the age of reason and it brought myth down from its solemn heights by blending it with fairy tale.

'The function of the central moral in fairy tales', writes the music historian David Buch, 'made them vehicles for Enlightenment allegory as well, where the "improvement" of the audience replaced that of the child'. The creators of grand opera in the eighteenth century weren't wrapped in nostalgia for lost hierarchy and solemnity, but forging a new, secular event that looks through the lens of wonder at all kinds of deep questions, about people and polities, passion and loyalty, power and fate. It invites our involvement to share in the predicaments it explores, some of them to do with myths' central concern—the place of humans in relation to mysteries of love and death. By a revealing paradox, Voltaire, the great rationalist, satirist, and sceptic, collaborated with the French composer Rameau on several (failed) operas. The counter-world of hopes and dreams that fairy tale summons is filled with marvels and illusions, which act as catalysts of a rational outcome, when harmony, justice, and mercy will prevail over threats from evil powers. A famous example is Mozart's *Singspiel*, *The Magic Flute*, an opera first performed in 1791, which combines allegory, comedy, and fairy tale, and culminates, after many ordeals for the protagonists, in rejoicing—at liberation from danger and happiness in love. Carter picks up on this exuberance in the last line of her last novel: 'What a joy it is to dance and sing!'

Because fairy tales can be meddled with, mixed up, and turned around in ways that an authored text resists, they have emerged as the favoured reservoir of contemporary mass entertainment, and their yields are in a perpetual state of metamorphosis. In 1890, when Adelheid Wette, the sister of the composer Engelbert Humperdinck, adapted the Grimms' *Hansel and Gretel* as a song cycle for her own family to perform at home at Christmas, she could not bear the cruelty of the Grimms' story, even in its watered-down version. She was alarmed, too, at how her children might react, and so she softened it—Gretel becomes motherly, Hansel protective and manly, and both say their prayers. The Sandman appears to lull the children to sleep and he's nothing like the terrifying figure of the Uncanny whom Freud discusses, but a benign angelic visitor who subdues the horrors of the scary dark forest.

This family Christmas concert eventually became her brother's much loved, magnificent opera, *Hansel and Gretel*. At the end, the children's parents come rushing onto the stage looking for them—they never meant to lose them, let alone expose them to die. All the witch's victims—who have been turned into gingerbread biscuits—come back to life. Joy and reassurance all round follows. Even the witch is revived out of the oven—in the form of a cake.

The young Humperdincks then, and children now at a panto or a play, might not already know the story—there is a first time in the dark forest, and they need to be held gently by the hand to meet the cruel mother and the greedy and punitive witch—often played as her double. For the first-time audience, fairy tales still have happy endings—and lots of comic business to lighten the threats.

Techno-Magic: Cinema and Fairy Tale

From the earliest experiments by George Meliès in Paris in the 1890s to the present day dominion of Disney Productions and Pixar, fairy tales have been told in the cinema. The concept of illusion carries two distinct, profound, and contradictory meanings in the medium of film: first, the film itself is an illusion, and, bar a few initiates screaming at the appearance of a moving train in the medium's earliest viewings, everyone in the cinema knows they are being stunned by wonders wrought by science. All appearances in the cinema are conjured by shadow play and artifice, and technologies ever more skilled at illusion: CGI produces living breathing simulacra—of velociraptors (*Jurassic Park*), elvish castles (*Lord of the Rings*), soaring bionic monsters (*Avatar*), grotesque and terrifying monsters (the *Alien* series), while the modern Rapunzel wields her mane like a lasso and a whip, or deploys it to make a footbridge. Such visualizations are designed to stun us, and they succeed: so much is being done for us by animators and filmmakers, there is no room for personal imaginings. The wicked queen in *Snow White* (1937) has become imprinted, and she keeps those exact features when we return to the story; Ariel, Disney's flame-haired Little Mermaid, has eclipsed her wispy and poignant predecessors, conjured chiefly by the words of Andersen's story.

A counterpoised form of illusion, however, now flourishes rampantly at the core of fairytale films, and has become central to the realization on screen of the stories, especially in entertainment which aims at a crossover or child audience. Contemporary commercial cinema has continued the Victorian shift from irresponsible amusement to responsible instruction, and kept faith with fairy tales' protest against existing injustices. Many current family films posit spirited, hopeful alternatives (in *Shrek* Princess Fiona is podgy, liverish, ugly, and delightful; in *Tangled*, Rapunzel is a super heroine, brainy and brawny; in the hugely successful Disney film *Frozen* (2013), inspired by *The Snow Queen*, the younger sister Anna overcomes ice storms, avalanches, and eternal winter to save Elsa, her elder). Screenwriters display iconoclastic verve, but they are working from the premise that screen illusions have power to become fact. 'Wishing on a star' is the ideology of the dream factory, and has given rise to indignant critique, that fairy tales peddle empty consumerism and wishful thinking. The writer Terri Windling, who specializes in the genre of teen fantasy, deplores the once prevailing tendency towards positive thinking and sunny success:

> The fairy tale journey may look like an outward trek across plains and mountains, through castles and forests, but the actual movement is inward, into the lands of the soul. The dark path of the fairytale forest lies in the shadows of our imagination, the depths of our unconscious. To travel to the wood, to face its dangers, is to emerge transformed by this experience. Particularly for children whose world does not resemble the simplified world of television sit-coms... this ability to travel inward, to face fear and transform it, is a

skill they will use all their lives. We do children—and ourselves—a grave disservice by censoring the old tales, glossing over the darker passages and ambiguities . . .

Fairy tale and film enjoy a profound affinity because the cinema animates phenomena, no matter how inert; made of light and motion, its illusions match the enchanted animism of fairy tale: animals speak, carpets fly, objects move and act of their own accord. One of the darker forerunners of Mozart's flute is an uncanny instrument that plays in several ballads and stories: a bone that bears witness to a murder. In the Grimms' tale, 'The Singing Bone', the shepherd who finds it doesn't react in terror and run, but thinks to himself, 'What a strange little horn, singing of its own accord like that. I must take it to the king.' The bone sings out the truth of what happened, and the whole skeleton of the victim is dug up, and his murderer—his elder brother and rival in love—is unmasked, sewn into a sack, and drowned.

This version is less than two pages long: a tiny, supersaturated solution of the Grimms: grotesque and macabre detail, uncanny dynamics of life-in-death, moral piety, and rough justice. But the story also presents a vivid metaphor for film itself: singing bones. (It's therefore apt, if a little eerie, that the celluloid from which film stock was first made was itself composed of rendered-down bones.)

Early animators' choice of themes reveals how they responded to a deeply laid sympathy between their medium of film and the uncanny vitality of inert things. Lotte Reiniger, the writer-director of the first full-length animated feature (*The Adventures of Prince Achmed*) (Figure 15), made dazzling 'shadow puppet' cartoons inspired by the

Figure 15 Oriental shadowplay: early animation takes its cue from the *Arabian Nights*. Aladdin and Dinarzade, from Lotte Reiniger, *The Adventures of Prince Achmed*, 1926.

fairy tales of Grimm, Andersen, and Wilhelm Hauff; she continued making films for over a thirty-year period, first in her native Berlin and later in London, for children's television. Her *Cinderella* (1922) is a comic—and grisly—masterpiece.

Early Disney films, made by the man himself, reflect traditional fables' personification of animals—mice and ducks and cats and foxes; in this century, by contrast, things come to life, no matter how inert they are: computerization observes no boundaries to generating lifelike, kinetic, cybernetic, and virtual reality.

BOX 6 *Living Toys*
....

L'Enfant et les Sortilèges (The Child and the Spells, 1925), was composed by Maurice Ravel to a libretto by the novelist Colette. In the opera, a cross and contrary child protagonist has a tantrum when his mother asks him if he has done his homework. He hasn't and he won't, so when she leaves him to it, he batters his toys, teases and torments his pet squirrel, smashes the teapot and teacup, slashes the curtains, swings on the pendulum of the grandfather clock, and pulls his cat's tail. When he tears up the pages of his book of fairy tales, the princess in the story appears to take her leave of him and he cries to keep her. All the while, the havoc he creates is mimicked vividly and wittily by the orchestra: the Wedgwood teapot and teacup jiggle to a ragtime tune; the Chinese cup steps to a foxtrot.

Colette and Ravel had a prophetic insight into an aspect of modern life, which Walt Disney would exploit to the full: the child's toys and his nursery furniture are not things, any more than his pets and other animals, but are living, conscious beings, independent of the child's make-believe. At the end, the naughty boy calls out for his mother, and his cry, 'Maman', is the Magic Word. With this summons, the opera ends in reconciliation and hope and love—like a classic fairy tale. The great puppeteer filmmaker Lotte Reiniger, who animated every kind of object through her art, tried valiantly to buy the rights to the opera, but failed. What a classic of fairytale film she would have made.

Utopian Dreams/Wishful Thinking

By far the most striking development in the alliance of fairy tale and cinema as vehicles in family entertainment has been the rise of political sensitivity, and resulting tinkering with stories to show awareness of gender, power relations, and ethnic representation. Both the cultural-historical and psychoanalytical approaches to fairy tale have sharpened producers' awareness of social engineering. Whereas Reiniger could show a jolly frolic in a harem, and Prince Achmed carousing with lascivious Josephine Baker-style houris, the writer and director of *Snow White and the Huntsman* (2012) could not even end the story with a marriage—to the prince or to the pauper. This Snow White (Kristen Stewart of the *Twilight* series) has to remain a lone heroine, a role model for the independent woman—at times in full armour. The rules of genre, which require some resolution to the story, were flouted in the interests of exemplary gender moulding.

Interestingly, the first experiments in character building through cinematic enchantments took place under socialist or communist regimes. The masters of Soviet Russia and the communist bloc demanded that artists and writers celebrate heroic workers, agricultural quotas, and the brotherhood of man; stray into dream and fantasy and you were dangerously flirting with a degenerate bourgeois aesthetic—veering close to the decadence of surrealism or the moral vacuity of subjective feeling. Many went to the Gulag for such personal flights of fancy.

But retelling fairy tales for a *child* audience could offer cover for alternative messages, and turn the official political programme for the arts topsy-turvy: tractors disappeared and flying carpets took over; golden fish swam into view and blue unicorns with long gold eyelashes pranced on the screen. Miracles happened that were not the result of five-year plans. From the Soviet Union, to Czechoslovakia and

Yugoslavia (as they were then called), the Grimms' founding principle—that fairy tale expressed the people and the nation—provided a rationale for dusting off traditional stories from all over the empire. Polishing them up for family viewing created a picture of joyous unity in diversity.

In the days when Stalin wanted everyone to be happy in the vast empire, fairy tales were collected, published (often in beautiful illustrated editions), and performed to forge community spirit. From Belgrade to Vladivostok, the Black Sea to the Arctic Ocean, ethnic stories were told, sung, acted—often in local national dress—to deepen the sense of belonging. Plots were fixed to give uplift: the brave little tailor rejects the princess in favour of the gardener's daughter; the greedybags treasure-hoarder is destroyed.

One of the most successful early fairytale films in colour, *The Singing Ringing Tree*, was made in 1957 in East Germany by the state-controlled studios, the DEFA. The story mashes many elements from favourite tales—several animal helpers, a wicked dwarf, a stuck-up princess, and a plucky, lowborn hero. Their struggles are epic, involving dark perils and terrifying trials. The tree itself reverberates with powerful magic, as in 'The Juniper Tree'. But these elements are slanted through the lens of East German politics: the proud, spoiled princess learns to love the people, makes common cause with the forces of righteousness, and leads a revolution against the dwarf.

Arguments did however flare up in East Germany around the use of fantasy and *The Singing Ringing Tree* in particular, and they sound very familiar. Why was the story about a princess at all? Why did it show her realizing the error of her arrogant ways? Surely this colluded reprehensibly with out-dated notions of reform and *noblesse oblige*? What about the happy ending when the princess and the pauper marry? Cries of 'bourgeois' and 'revanchist!' echoed round the bureaux of the censors.

The series was pulled, mothballed and forgotten—its makers were embarrassed to recall it when later asked by enthusiastic fans. But in 1962, the BBC bought the film—and sparked unforgettable thrills in a generation of British children, and continued enthusiasm among film buffs.

The East German case is highly illuminating of present tensions around the telling of fairy tales. On the one hand, the general consensus now agrees with Dickens, Tolkien, Bettelheim, and Windling, who, for different reasons, have declared that sweetening the tales is tantamount to vandalism. But at the same time, changes to the corpus are constantly being made in the light of current opinion—muting and muffling this bit or that—without any official censors needing to be brought in.

The kind of political wishful thinking that emanated from the old Soviet bloc resembles what is called PC or political correctness, which is often scorned, and perhaps applied to extremes. Yet it depends on recognizing that what we discover in books or other media when we are young imprints us—stories communicate values, like myths, and shape our understanding of the world.

One of the consequences has been the rise of self-censorship—by publishers, producers, scriptwriters, and editors, most especially when children are in view. Behind every book for young people and every global product of family entertainment, the hum of boardroom discussion about the politics of the work can be heard. Every scriptwriter and director takes up a passive Cinderella and turns her into a champion freedom fighter, or transforms Jack the Giant Killer into Robin Hood, in order to put across an approved code of conduct—the values that will win approval and ratings. The big film industry ('Hollywood') keeps straining to produce a fairytale heroine for the age of the female CEO, but its efforts fall foul of audiences and are still arousing fierce attacks from children's experts in every field.

One consequence of twenty-first-century social and political sensitivities has been a clear split in some cases between material for children and adults, similar to the division between top-shelf and eye-level magazines on a news stand or the two sides of the 9 p.m. watershed in television broadcasting. Many fairytale re-visionings now require Parental Guidance; several are classified Adults Only.

Current fairy tales on stage and screen reveal an acute malaise about sexual, rather than social, programming of the female, and the genre continues ever more intensively to wrestle with the notorious question Freud put long ago, 'What do women want?' The singer Tori Amos, for example, adapted a Victorian fairy tale, *The Light Princess* (2013), about a girl who has lost her gravity—she has to be tethered to prevent her floating up and away and she can't do anything but laugh. George MacDonald wrote the original tale in 1867; he was a Christian allegorist, a friend of Lewis Carroll's, and encouraged and influenced the *Alice* books. Tori Amos's vision, by contrast, is sparked by the dominant, psychological concern today with young girls' troubles and unfocused desires, the search for numbness and nullity that leads to binge drinking, passing out, self-harm, even death.

The popularity of different fairy tales beats with an irregular pulse: recurrent favourites are 'Snow White' and 'Sleeping Beauty', with 'Bluebeard' coming close behind. The idea that women must stop sleepwalking through life has its origins in feminist anger against the Sleeping Beauty ideal (think of *The Stepford Wives*), but the concern is spiking (Disney's *Maleficent* (2014) stars Angelina Jolie in the title role as the thirteenth fairy; the brilliantly inventive choreographer Matthew Bourne has turned Sleeping Beauty's prince into a vampire, who wakes her with a bite...the fairy tale seen through *Twilight*). *Blancanieves* (2012), made in Spain, is an exhilarating, inspired reinvention of 'Snow White', set among the flamenco dancers, bullfighters, and travelling circus folk of Andalusia. Directed and written by the Catalan director Pablo Berger, it is shot in expressionist chiaroscuro, and gorgeously controlled, with a play of shimmer and glare on mirrors, crystal, eyes, and lips in the stark sunlight of the bullring and the deep shadows of interiors, castles, caravans.

No compunction about depicting evil restrains the storyteller here: the wicked stepmother is a nurse who sees her chance when the gored hero of the bullring is admitted to her hospital, his wife dies in childbirth, and he is left paralysed; nothing is spared to show us her cruelty, vanity, greed—no plot lines are added to excuse her, in contrast to the Hollywood vehicles, for which scriptwriters are made to come up with back stories of trauma to soften her evil. Maribel Verdú, the actress playing the wicked queen

Figure 16 'Are you afraid of being poisoned?': the wicked queen in modern dress. Maribel Verdú as the wicked stepmother in Pablo Berger's film, *Blancanieves*, 2012.

(Figure 16), has an uncanny face that changes, with a twitch of her lips, from glorious serene diva to predatory fury, and she gives Berger's dominatrix a marvellous, witty energy, on the verge of parody, but always remaining too threatening to allow the release of laughter.

Like many current fairytale films, this one is not for children, but uses the famous children's story to think about what can happen to innocence. *Blancanieves* adopts the full awareness of adults, and shows us openly what adults are capable of in the fulfilment of desire—especially perverse desire.

The film is a tragedy, for this Snow White falls asleep forever and, as in Kafka's 'The Hunger Artist', she is exhibited in her glass coffin as part of a travelling fair, alongside a hairy girl, a fat lady, and a starveling. It's another form of Buñuel-style erotic fetishism, and the dwarf who loves her tends her with powder and paint; the film closes on a single tear leaking out of the corner of her eye.

The most disquieting treatment of the story is however a self-identified feminist film, Julia Leigh's *Sleeping Beauty* (2011), which exemplifies the dark turn fairy tales have taken, especially in the vision of women creators. A luminous, angelically beautiful student answers a job advert and is initiated into a specialist brothel, willingly becoming the drugged object of clients' fantasies. Like Carter's essay *The Sadeian Woman*, this version raises questions about women's complicity and self-possession, and about pornography as the norm of sexual exchange in our society, not an aberration.

Recognizing the dark heart of fairy tales has informed some stunning original works: *Pan's Labyrinth* (2006), directed and written by Guillermo del Toro, condenses many myths into his story, about the goddess Persephone abducted into the underworld, for example. The film opens with a direct allusion to the 'Cottingley fairies', when two little girls persuaded Conan Doyle and other eminent Victorians that they had seen—and successfully photographed—tiny sprites dancing and sunbathing at the bottom of their garden, and it then unfolds into a searing tale of initiation in the gloomy forest, brilliantly weaving the actual historical reality of Spain under Franco into the fabric of magic and faery.

Many of the most widespread and powerful expressions of fairy tale today feature women—old and young—at their heart. Whether the creators are male (*Tangled*, for example, has a male screenwriter and director), or female (*Maleficent* is written by Linda Woolverton, also the screenwriter on Disney's *Beauty and the Beast*), readers and viewers, regardless of their gender, are drawn into the unfolding drama about a passionate female protagonist. Although Hollywood keeps trying to bring appealing young men into the picture (*Snow White and the Huntsman* struggled to make the male lead hunky *and* sensitive), Harry Potter stands pretty much alone among heroes, and J. K. Rowling's series is too baggy and epic to be called a fairy tale.

Twenty-first century films, such as *Sleeping Beauty* and *Blancanieves*, have broken with the chief defining principle of fairy tales that they should end happily. Fairy tales lift the spirits and spark a ray of hope for the future when they bring defeat and even death to the perpetrators of harm, to the vicious tyrants and greedy ogres and to the architects of family hell, cruel fathers and wicked queens. The darkness of contemporary retellings threatens to grow so deep it throws a shadow over the happy ending itself. But sometimes this gloom does not altogether destroy the sense that an alternative world has been created where goodness can brighten us, lighten us.

EPILOGUE

> The kingdom of fairy tales...could be ecstasy but it is above all a land of pathos, of symbols of pain.
>
> Cristina Campo

In *The Servant's Tale* by the American writer Paula Fox, the author's childhood self asks, '"What's the difference between a story and a lie?"' Her Nana replies 'impatiently: "A lie hides the truth, a story tries to find it."' The little girl strains 'to grasp her meaning..."Don't worry," she said soothingly. "You'll see it all someday."'

Paula Fox then adds, 'I understood enough to know that Nana saw what others couldn't see, that for her the meaning of one thing could also be the meaning of a greater thing.'

Fairy tales are stories that try to find the truth and give us glimpses of the greater things—this is the principle that underlies their growing presence in writing, art, cinema, dance, song. The tales used to be light in the midst of darkness. But dislike of shallow promises and easy solutions in times of conflict, eco-disaster, and other difficulties are clipping the wings of the fairy tale; hope can seem a deliberate falsehood. Disneyfication has become a dirty word—synonymous with mendacity—though it's not altogether the case that his early films are so saccharine or sanitized as charged. The 'realisation of imagined wonder', which Tolkien saw as the aim of fairy tale, isn't bright and shiny any more; its skies have clouded over. The stories used to be distinct from epic and tragedy, but renderings today are moving closer to those forms of storytelling. A few dissenting voices still consider fairy tales childish and foolish, but on the whole, they have been widely accepted as a most valuable and profound creation of human history and culture; they have come to be treated as scriptures from an authentic inaugural time of imaginative activity, a narrative blueprint when it was all set down, right and true.

For these reasons, fairy tales are gradually turning into myths: stories held in common about the deepest dilemmas, no longer aiming at being optimistic or consoling, but rather bearers of wisdom, deep, thought-provoking, and illuminating. Maria Tatar writes about 'the ignition power' of fairy tales, 'the ability to kindle our powers of imagination so that the mind's eye begins to see scenes created by mere words on the page', and with this vivid summons of hitherto unknown dimensions of experience, the world of faerie stimulates sensations and emotions—fear, pleasure, dread, gratification. The most difficult task has now become how to make a story of child abandonment and cannibal witches bearable for small children at Christmas, as well as for those older and more knowing, in order to keep faith with the truth-telling inside the stories. Increasingly, the tendency now is to leave them to us, the grown-ups.

We are walking through the dark forest, trying to spot the breadcrumbs and follow the path. But the birds have eaten them, and we are on our own. Now is the time when we all must become trackers and readers of signs. Fairy tales give us something to go on. It's not much, but it'll have to do. It is something to start with.

FURTHER READING

GENERAL

Benjamin, Walter, 'The Storyteller: Reflections on the Works of Nikolai Leskov', in *Illuminations*, ed. Hannah Arendt, trans. Harry Zohn (London: Fontana, 1973).

Bloom, Harold, ed., *The Hero's Journey* (New York: Infobase, 2009).

Borges, Jorge Luis, *Other Inquisitions, 1937–1953* (Austin, Tex.: University of Texas Press, 1964).

Calvino, Italo, *Italian Folktales*, trans. George Martin (New York: Harcourt Brace Jovanovich, 1980).

Calvino, Italo, *Sulla Fiaba*, ed. Mario Lavagetto (Turin: Einaudi, 1988).

Dasen, Véronique, and Hennard Dutheil de la Rochère, Martine, *Des Fata aux fées*: *regards croisés de l'Antiquité à nos jours* (Lausanne: University of Lausanne, 2011).

Davidson, Hilda Ellis and Anna Chaudhri, *A Companion to the Fairy Tale* (Cambridge: D.S. Brewer, 2003).

Féeries: Etudes sur le conte merveilleux XVIIe–XIXe siècle (Université Stendhal-Grenoble), 2003–.

Gramarye: The Journal of the Sussex Centre for Folklore, Fairy Tales and Fantasy, 2012– .

Haase, Donald, ed., *The Greenwood Encyclopedia of Folktales and Fairy Tales*, Vols. I–III (Westport, Conn.: Greenwood Press, 2008).

Heaney, Seamus, *The Redress of Poetry* (London: Faber & Faber, 2011).

Lewis, C. S., *Of Other Worlds: Essays and Stories*, ed. Walter Hooper (London: Geoffrey Bles, 1966).

Lewis, C. S., *Selected Literary Essays*, ed. Walter Hooper (Cambridge: Cambridge University Press, 1969).

Lüthi, Max, *The Fairy Tale as Art Form and the Nature of Man*, trans. Jon Erickson (Oxford: Wiley & Sons, 1987).

Marvels and Tales: Journal of Fairy-Tale Studies (Detroit: Wayne State University Press).

Ouyang, Wen-chin, ed., *The Arabian Nights* (London: Everyman, 2014).

Propp, Vladimir, *Morphology of the Folk-Tale* (Austin, Tex.: University of Texas).

Salmon, Christian, *Storytelling: Bewitching the Modern Mind*, trans. David Macey (London and New York: Verso, 2010).

Tatar, Maria, ed., *The Classic Fairy Tales* (New York and London: W.W. Norton & Co., 1999).

Teverson, Andrew, *Fairy Tale (The New Critical Idiom)* (London: Routledge, 2013).

Tiffin, Jessica, *Marvellous Geometry: Genre and Metafiction in Modern Fairy Tale* (Detroit: Wayne State University Press, 2009).

Tolkien, J. R. R., *Tree and Leaf* (London: Allen & Unwin, 1964).

Warner, Marina, *From the Beast to the Blonde: On Fairy Tales and their Tellers* (London: Chatto & Windus, 1994).

Warner, Marina, *No Go the Bogeyman: Scaring, Lulling and Making Mock* (London: Chatto & Windus, 1998).

Warner, Marina, ed., *Wonder Tales* (London: Chatto & Windus, 1996).

Warnes, Chris, *Magical Realism and the Postcolonial Novel: Between Faith and Irreverence* (London: Palgrave, 2009).

Zipes, Jack, trans., *Beauties, Beasts and Enchantments: Classic French Fairy Tales* (New York: NAL Books, 1989).

Zipes, Jack, ed., *The Oxford Companion to Fairy Tales: The Western Fairy Tale Tradition from Medieval to Modern* (Oxford: Oxford University Press, 2000).

Zipes, Jack, ed., *The Great Fairy Tale Tradition: From Straparola and Basile to the Brothers Grimm* (New York and London: W.W. Norton & Co., 2001).

Zipes, Jack, *Fairy Tales and the Art of Subversion*, 2nd edn. (New York and London: Routledge, 2006).

Zipes, Jack, *The Irresistible Fairy Tale: The Cultural and Social History of a Genre* (Princeton: Princeton University Press, 2012).

PROLOGUE

Borges, Jorge Luis, *Labyrinths*, ed. Donald A. Yates and James E. Irby (London: Penguin, 1964).

Duffy, Carol Ann, Still, Melly, and Supple, Tim, *Beasts and Beauties*, dir. Melly Still, Hampstead Theatre, December 2011–January 2012.

CHAPTER 1. THE WORLDS OF FAERY:
FAR AWAY & DOWN BELOW

Auden, W. H., *Forewords and Afterwords* (New York: Vintage, 1974).

Barrie, J. M., *The Annotated Peter Pan*, ed. Maria Tatar (New York and London: W.W. Norton 2011).

Borges, Jorge Luis, *The Book of Imaginary Beings*, trans. Norman Thomas di Giovanni (London: Vintage, 2002).

Briggs, Katharine, *The Anatomy of Puck: An Examination of Fairy Beliefs among Shakespeare's Contemporaries and Successors* (London: Routledge & Kegan Paul, 1959).

Garner, Alan, ed., *A Book of Goblins* (London: Penguin, 1969).

Hunter, Michael, ed., *The Occult Laboratory: Magic, Science and Second Sight in Late 17th-Century Scotland* (Woodbridge: Boydell Books, 2001).

Jolles, André, *Einfache Formen: Legende/Sage/Mythe/Spruch Kasus/Memorabile/Märchen/Witz* (Darmstadt: Wissenschaftliche Buchgesellshaft, 1958).

Keightley, Thomas, *The Fairy Mythology Illustrative of the Romance and Superstition of Various Countries* (London: George Bell & Sons, 1910).

Kirk, Robert, *The Secret Commonwealth of Elves, Fauns, and Fairies*, with intro. by Marina Warner (New York: New York Review Books, 2009).

Paracelsus (Theophrastus van Hohenheim), *Four Treatises*, inc. *A Book on Nymphs, Sylphs, Pygmies*, etc., ed. and trans. E. Sigerest (Baltimore: Johns Hopkins Press, 1996).

CHAPTER 2. WITH A TOUCH OF HER WAND:
MAGIC & METAMORPHOSIS

Bell, Karl, *The Legend of Spring-Heeled Jack: Victorian Urban Folklore and Popular Cultures* (Woodbridge: The Boydell Press, 2012).

Carter, Angela, *The Bloody Chamber and Other Stories* (London: Victor Gollancz, 1979).

Carter, Angela, ed., *The Virago Book of Fairy Tales*, intro. by Marina Warner (London: Virago, 1990).

Chandler, Robert, *The Magic Ring and Other Russian Folktales* (London: Faber & Faber, 1979).

Coover, Robert, *Briar Rose and Spanking the Maid* (London: Penguin, 1996).

Crossley-Holland, Kevin, *Folk-Tales of the British Isles* (London: Faber & Faber, 1985).

Ellis, John M., *One Fairy Story Too Many: The Brothers Grimm and Their Tales* (Chicago: University of Chicago Press, 1983).

Gonzenbach, Laura, *Beautiful Angiola: The Lost Sicilian Folk and Fairy Tales of Laura Gonzenbach*, ed. and trans. Jack Zipes (New York: Routledge, 2003).

Gonzenbach, Laura, *The Robber with a Witch's Head*, ed. and trans. Jack Zipes (New York: Routledge, 2004).

Grimm, Jacob and Wilhelm, *Selected Tales*, trans. Joyce Crick (Oxford: Oxford University Press, 2005).

Grimm, Jacob and Wilhelm, *The Complete Fairy Tales of the Brothers Grimm*, trans. Jack Zipes (Toronto and London: Bantam Books, 1987).

Hennard Dutheil de la Rochère, Martine, *Reading, Translating, Rewriting: Angela Carter's Translational Poetics* (Detroit: Wayne State University Press, 2013).

Pullman, Philip, *Grimm Tales: For Young and Old* (London: Penguin, 2012).

Straparola, Giovan Francesco, *The Pleasant Nights*, ed. Donald Beecher, trans. W. G. Waters, 2 vols. (Toronto and London: University of Toronto Press, 2012).

Tatar, Maria, ed., *The Annotated Brothers Grimm* (New York and London: W.W. Norton & Co., 2004).

Warner, Marina, *Fantastic Metamorphoses, Other Worlds* (Oxford: Oxford University Press, 2001).

Warner, Marina, *Stranger Magic: Charmed States and the Arabian Nights* (London: Chatto & Windus, 2012).

CHAPTER 3. VOICES ON THE PAGE: TALES, TELLERS & TRANSLATORS

Afanasyev, A. N., *Russian Fairy Tales*, trans. Norbert Guterman, intro. by Roman Jakobson (New York: Random House, c.1973).

Balázs, Béla, *The Cloak of Dreams: Chinese Fairy Tales*, trans. Jack Zipes (Princeton: Princeton University Press, 2010).

Basile, Giambattista, *The Pentameron*, trans. Sir Richard Burton (London: William Kimber, 1952).

Basile, Giambattista, *Il racconto dei racconti, ovvero Il trattenimento dei piccoli,* trans. Ruggero Guarini , eds. Alessandra Burani and Ruggero Guarini (Milan: Adelphi Edizioni, 1994).

Calvino, Italo, *Fiabe Italiane*, 2 vols. (Turin: Einaudi, 1956).

Calvino, Italo, *Italian Folktales*, trans. George Martin (London: Penguin, 1980).

Canepa, Nancy, ed., *Out of the Woods: The Origins of the Literary Fairy Tale in Italy and France* (Detroit: Wayne State University Press, 1998).

Čapek, Karel, *Nine Fairy Tales*, trans. Dagmar Herrmann (Evanston, Ill.: Northwestern University Press, 1990).

D'Aulnoy, Madame, *Contes*, ed. Philippe Hourcade. Vol. I: *Les Contes des Fées*; Vol. II: *Contes nouveaux ou Les Fées à la Mode* (Paris: Société des Textes Français Modernes, 1997).

Dupont, Florence, *The Invention of Literature: From Greek Intoxication to the Latin Book*, trans. Janet Lloyd (Baltimore: Johns Hopkins University Press, 1999).

Grimm, Jacob and Wilhelm, *German Popular Stories*, ed. and trans. Edgar Taylor, illus. George Cruikshank [1823] (London: The Scholar Press, 1977), 2 Vols.

Haase, Donald, ed., *The Reception of Grimms' Fairy Tales: Responses, Reactions, Revisions* (Detroit: Wayne State University Press, 1993).

Hannon, Patricia, *Fabulous Identities: Women's Fairy Tales in Seventeenth-Century France* (Amsterdam and Atlanta, Ga.: Rodopi, 1998).

Jacobs, Joseph, ed., *Celtic Fairy Tales* (London: Senate, 1994).

Lang, Andrew, ed., *The Green Fairy Book* (New York: Dover Publications, 1965 [1892]). (And others in the series.)

Maitland, Sara, *Gossip from the Forest: The Tangled Roots of Our Forests and Fairytales* (London: Granta, 2012).

Perrault, Charles, *The Fairy Tales of Charles Perrault*, trans. Angela Carter (London: Penguin, 2008).

Perrault, Charles, *The Complete Fairy Tales*, trans. Christopher Betts (Oxford: Oxford University Press, 2009).

Spufford, Francis, *The Child that Books Built: A Memoir of Childhood and Reading* (London: Faber, 2002).

Winterson, Jeanette, *The Passion* (London: Bloomsbury, 1987).

Zipes, Jack, *The Original Folk and Fairy Tales of the Brothers Grimm: The Complete First Edition* (Princeton: Princeton University Press, 2014).

CHAPTER 4. POTATO SOUP: TRUE STORIES/REAL LIFE

Barzilai, Shuli, *Tales of Bluebeard and His Wives from Late Antiquity to Postmodern Times* (New York and London: Routledge, 2009).

Darnton, Robert, *The Great Cat Massacre: And Other Episodes in French Cultural History* (London: Allen Lane, 1984).

Hermansson, Casie E., *Bluebeard: A Reader's Guide to the English Tradition* (Jackson, Miss.: University Press of Mississippi, 2009).

Philip, Neil, *The Cinderella Story: The Origins and Variations of the Story Known as 'Cinderella'* (London: Penguin, 1989).

Pollock, Griselda, and Anderson, Victoria (eds.), *Bluebeard's Legacy: Death and Secrets From Bartók to Hitchcock* (London and New York: I.B. Tauris, 2009).

Tatar, Maria, *The Hard Facts of the Grimms' Fairy Tales* (Princeton: Princeton University Press, 1987).

Weber, Eugen, 'Fairies and Hard Facts: The Reality of Folktales', *Journal of the History of Ideas*, Vol. 42, No. 1 (Jan.–Mar. 1981).

CHAPTER 5. CHILDISH THINGS: PICTURES & CONVERSATIONS

Carroll, Lewis, *Alice's Adventures in Wonderland* and *Through the Looking-Glass*, ed. Hugh Haughton (London: Penguin, 2003).

Grimm, Jacob and Wilhelm, *German Popular Stories*, ed. and trans. Edgar Taylor, illus. George Cruikshank [1823] (London: The Scolar Press, 1977), 2 Vols.

Handler Spitz, Ellen, *Inside Picture Books* (New Haven: Yale University Press, 1999).

The History of Little Goody Two-Shoes (London: John Newbery, 1765).

Hockney, David, *Six Fairy Tales* (London: Petersburg Press, 1970).

Makdisi, Saree, and Nussbaum, Felicity, eds., *The Arabian Nights in Historical Context* (Oxford: Oxford University Press, 2008).

Sendak, Maurice, *Caldecott & Co: Notes on Books and Pictures* (London: Reinhardt Books, 1988).

Sumpter, Caroline, *The Victorian Press and the Fairy Tale* (Basingstoke: Palgrave Macmillan, 2012).

Uglow, Jenny, *Words and Pictures: Writers, Artists and a Peculiarly British Tradition* (London: Faber, 2012).

CHAPTER 6. ON THE COUCH: HOUSE-TRAINING THE ID

Bettelheim, Bruno, *The Uses of Enchantment: The Meaning and Importance of Fairy Tales* (London: Thames & Hudson, 1976).

Bly, Robert, *Iron John: A Book about Men* (Shaftesbury: Element Books, 1991).

Frank, Arthur W., *Letting Stories Breathe: A Socio-Narratology* (Chicago and London: University of Chicago Press, 2010).

Freud, Sigmund, 'The "Uncanny"', in Sigmund Freud, *Art and Literature*, Vol. 14 of *The Penguin Freud Library*, ed. and trans. James Strachey (London: Penguin, 1990).

Hoffmann, E. T. A., *The Best Tales of Hoffmann*, ed. E. F. Bleiler (New York: Dover Publications, Inc., 1967).

Mavor, Carol, *Reading Boyishly: Roland Barthes, J. M. Barrie, Jacques-Henri Lartigue, Marcel Proust, and D. W. Winnicott* (Durham, NC: Duke University Press, 2008).

Sexton, Anne, *Transformations* (New York: Houghton Mifflin, 1971).

Stephenson, Craig E., *Possession: Jung's Comparative Anatomy of the Psyche* (London: Routledge, 2009).

CHAPTER 7. IN THE DOCK: DON'T BET ON THE PRINCE

Adam, Helen, *A Helen Adam Reader*, ed. Kristin Prevallet (Orono, Me.: The National Poetry Foundation, 2007).

Bernheimer, Kate, ed., *Mirror, Mirror on the Wall: Women Writers Explore Their Favorite Fairy Tales* (New York: Anchor Books, 1998).

Bottigheimer, Ruth B., *Grimms' Bad Girls and Bold Boys: The Moral and Social Vision of the Tales* (New Haven: Yale University Press, 1987).

Carter, Angela, *The Sadeian Woman: An Exercise in Cultural History* (London: Virago, 1979).

Chase, Richard, *The Jack Tales* (New York: Houghton Mifflin, 1943).

Figes, Eva, *Tales of Innocence and Experience: An Exploration* (London: Bloomsbury, 2003).

Franz, Marie Louise von, *Problems of the Feminine in Fairytales* (Dallas, Tex.: Spring Publications, Inc., 1972).

Gilbert, Sandra M., and Gubar, Susan, *The Madwoman in the Attic: The Woman Writer and the Nineteenth-Century Literary Imagination*, 2nd edn. (New Haven: Yale University Press, 1984 [1979]).

Haase, Donald (ed.), *Fairy Tales and Feminism: New Approaches* (Detroit: Wayne State University Press, 2004).

Sage, Lorna, ed., *Flesh and the Mirror: Essays on the Art of Angela Carter* (London: Virago, 1994).

Zipes, Jack, *Don't Bet on the Prince: Contemporary Feminist Fairy Tales in North America and England* (New York: Gower, 1986).

CHAPTER 8. DOUBLE VISION: THE DREAM OF REASON

Bacchilega, Cristina, *Postmodern Fairy Tales: Gender and Narrative Strategies* (Philadelphia: University of Pennsylvania Press, 1997).

Borges, Jorge Luis, *Collected Fictions*, trans. Andrew Hurley (London: Penguin, 1999).

Borges, Jorge Luis, *The Total Library: Non-Fiction (1922–1986)*, ed. Eliot Weinberger, trans. Esther Allen et al. (London: Penguin, 2007).

Bridgwater, Patrick, *Kafka, Gothic and Fairy Tale* (Amsterdam: Rodopi, 2003).

Calvino, Italo, *The Complete Cosmicomix*, trans. Martin McLaughlin, Tim Parks, and William Weaver (London: Penguin Books, 2010).

Calvino, Italo, *If on a Winter's Night a Traveller*, trans. William Weaver (London and New York: Harcourt Brace Jovanovich, 1981).

Calvino, Italo, *Invisible Cities*, trans. William Weaver (London: Secker & Warburg, 1974).

Calvino, Italo, *Six Memos for the Next Millennium*, trans. Patrick Creagh (London: Jonathan Cape, 1992).

Carter, Angela, *Burning Your Boats: Stories* (London: Chatto & Windus, 1995).

Carter, Angela, *Nights at the Circus* (London: Chatto & Windus, The Hogarth Press, 1984).

Carter Angela, *Wise Children* (London: Chatto & Windus, 1991).

Kafka, Franz, *The Complete Short Stories*, ed. Nahum N. Glatzer, trans. Martin Secker (London: Vintage, 1999).

McAra, Catriona, and Calvin, David, eds., *Anti-Tales: The Uses of Disenchantment* (Newcastle: Cambridge Scholars, 2011).

Schwitters, Kurt, *Lucky Hans and Other Merz Fairy Tales*, trans. Jack Zipes (Princeton: Princeton University Press, 2009).

Ugrešić, Dubravka, *Baba Yaga Laid an Egg*, trans. Ellen Elias-Bursác, Celia Hawkesworth, and Mark Thompson (Edinburgh: Canongate, 2009).

CHAPTER 9. ON STAGE & SCREEN: STATES OF ILLUSION

Balina, Marina, Goscilo, Helena, and Lipovetsky, Mark, eds., *Politicizing Magic: An Anthology of Russian and Soviet Fairy Tales* (Evanston, Ill.: Northwestern University Press, 2005).

Buch, David J., *Magic Flutes and Enchanted Forests* (Chicago: University of Chicago Press, 2008).

Giroux, Henry A., *The Mouse that Roared: Disney and the End of Innocence* (Lanham, Md.: Rowman & Littlefield, 1999).

Nelson, Victoria, *Gothicka: Vampire Heroes, Human Gods, and the New Supernatural* (Cambridge, Mass. and London: Harvard University Press, 2012).

Zipes, Jack, *Happily Ever After: Fairy Tales, Children, and the Culture Industry* (New York and London: Routledge, 1997).

EPILOGUE

Campo, Cristina, *Gli Imperdonabili* (Milan: Adelphi, 1987).

Fox, Paula, *A Servant's Tale* (San Francisco: Virago, 1984).

Tatar, Maria, *Enchanted Hunters: The Power of Stories in Childhood* (New York: W.W. Norton & Co., 2009).

PUBLISHER'S ACKNOWLEDGEMENTS

We are grateful for permission to include the following copyright material in this book.

Quotation from Helen Adam, 'Down There in the Dark', copyright © the Literary Estate of Helen Adam as administered by the Poetry Collection of the University Libraries, University at Buffalo, The State University of New York, and reproduced with permission.

Excerpt from 'Cinderella' from TRANSFORMATIONS by Anne Sexton. Copyright © 1971 by Anne Sexton. Copyright © renewed by 1999 by Linda G. Sexton. Reprinted by permission of Houghton Mifflin Harcourt Publishing Company. All rights reserved.

Excerpt from 'Briar Rose (Sleeping Beauty)' from TRANSFORMATIONS by Anne Sexton. Copyright © renewed by 1999 by Linda G. Sexton. Reprinted by permission of Houghton Mifflin Harcourt Publishing Company. All rights reserved.

INDEX

Note: **Bold** entries refer to illustrations.